Fly Fishing
for
Big Pike

Fly Fishing
for
Big Pike

ALAN HANNA

First edition December 1998
Published by Coch-y-Bonddu Books, Machynlleth.
Copyright Alan Hanna 1998.

ISBN 0 9533 648 1X

This edition limited to five hundred copies only.

Published & distributed by
COCH-Y-BONDDU BOOKS,
MACHYNLLETH, POWYS, SY20 8DJ
Tel 01654 702837   Fax 01654 702857

CONTENTS

ACKNOWLEDGEMENTS

This book owes its origins to my gifted friend, Johnny Saunderson. Not only did he make a timely suggestion to write the book, but he generously assisted with the project by taking some of the photographs, as well as accompanying me on many a fishing trip.

I am greatly indebted to John Todd, who, right from the outset of our friendship, behaved with a generosity befitting a life-long friend. John is one of Northern Ireland's premier game angling ghillies - (his client list is very impressive!) - and from time to time he has introduced me to some of the 'big guns' of the angling world. (He's on 01232 862419 if you're planning a visit!)

Thanks also to Jonny Phenix, whose creative ingenuity and endless enthusiasm has never failed to inspire and encourage me.

Frankie McPhillips, fly tying supremo, who kindly agreed to tie Ballydoolagh Bombers for customers who wish to purchase 'off the shelf' flies. A real gentleman, to be sure.

To Paul Morgan, of Coch-y-bonddu Books, who remained positive throughout the project, and whose tactful suggestions greatly improved the manuscript. Another real gentleman, to be sure, (or whatever they say in Wales.)

Most of all, however, I extend my thanks to Jolanda, my wife, without whose generosity, support, and persistent optimism lots of things wouldn't get done - including this book!

INTRODUCTION

I was playing host to the great American fly-fisher Ed Jaworowski, who was making his first visit to Northern Ireland, and in the planning stage I had asked my pal John Todd whether he could arrange someone to take Ed pike fly-fishing.

"I'll ask Alan Hanna", John replied. "And I'll ask him to take Ed fly-fishing for pollack as well".

The first day was pollack fishing, and through Alan's guidance Ed added yet another species to his huge list of fish caught on the fly. The next day we met Alan by a small lough close to his home town of Enniskillen. John and I watched as Alan launched his little boat, and as Ed's not inconsequential frame lowered itself into the stern seat, leaving about two inches of dry fibreglass above the water-line. As they began to cast out their pike flies in the direction of a sparse reed-bed, the action took the stern to within a hair's breadth of being submerged. I closed my eyes and prayed that they could both swim. John and I had then to return to town to buy some provisions. We returned two hours later to find that the Irish and American experts had already accounted for nineteen pike, and lost a few including one very big one.

I watched Alan fish: his casting style is excellent and effortless. His understanding of loughs and pike second to none. His pike flies are very effective. We talked: it became clear that this quiet man had a fund of untapped knowledge and understanding based, not on second-hand information, but on vast experience borne of long days of fishing.

You will find much of this knowledge and understanding set out in this book.

Malcolm Greenhalgh

CHAPTER 1

The Provocative Pike

I have often wondered what it is about the pike that provokes such strong feelings in so many anglers. In some, the pike fosters an obsessive interest to the exclusion of all other species, while in others the poor pike generates a vociferous loathing that creates lifelong enemies.

I suppose this is not so surprising when one considers how emphatically the pike nails its colours to the mast. No concerns here for beauty or compromise: the pike is a lean, mean, killing machine - a predator through and through. Therein, I think, lies the source of much of the hostility which the pike attracts, as well as much of the interest.

I am convinced, though, that far more people secretly admire the pike than will admit to it. Most freshwater anglers have, at some stage in their angling careers, had a desire to tangle with *Esox lucius*, the king of British coarse fish. The fact that I have yet to meet a small boy with a fishing rod who hasn't dreamt of catching a big pike is confirmation enough of the widespread interest among anglers in this species, even if it is dormant in (or denied by!) many of them. All anglers are hunters by definition, and most of us possess at least a grudging respect for this hunter par excellence.

My own angling career started out with an insatiable lust for those teeth and that power. However, a few years - and a fortune's worth of spoon baits - later, (and only a handful of pike!), I was introduced to the gentle and skilful art of river fly fishing, and the hunt for 'Jaws' was relegated to the second division.

That is, until one fateful day, when I was taken by surprise while fly fishing at Horton, near London. Horton is an excellent mixed fishery and I was teasing an Ace of Spades under some trees in search of a big brown trout when it was seized by something huge. Horton has a population of big pike, and when the line suddenly went dead (after having had the rod nearly pulled out of my hand!) I knew immediately what had happened. Sure enough, the fly was gone, and the six pound leader neatly sliced through by those pin-sharp teeth. This experience inspired many fly tying experiments in the ensuing months and years, but my best efforts enjoyed only limited success.

I did not really crack it until recently. After many years of trying, I have finally developed a method of catching pike on rod and fly that is really successful - and I mean *really* successful. It is far more productive than most other methods in common use, and it comes into its own on those days when pike seemingly refuse to look at anything. But best of all, it regularly produces big pike, the kind of fish which are mostly taken on livebait or ledgered deadbait.

This book will, I think, appeal to two distinct - and very different - types of angler. If you are a confirmed pike addict looking for a new approach to your sport, then you are about to discover what I believe to be one of the most productive and sporting methods of catching pike. Not only that, it is the most exhilarating way to take pike on rod and line - by a considerable margin.

This book will also appeal to the established fly fisherman who wants to expand his horizons by seeking out new challenges. I suspect there are many who fit this bill, as it is only too common these days for anglers to grow tired of catching fat trout from stocked ponds week after week.

Either way, there is enormous satisfaction to be gained from catching pike on fly rod and line, and this book will tell you how.

CHAPTER 2

THE SPORTING ADVANTAGES OF FLY-FISHING

Fly fishing, I am told, is the fastest growing sector of angling in Britain today. Yet it involves the most simple of all fishing tackle. In this world of hi-tech aids and appliances, it is interesting - and very pleasing - to note that the simplest approach is gaining the most ground. I think this tells us something about the appeal and mystique of fishing in general. The hunting instinct does not want to be satisfied easily - it demands the hunt. The more skill and ingenuity required to catch the quarry, the more satisfying is the success. Make it too easy and the angler will quickly lose interest.

This partly explains the growing interest in fly fishing. There is something very gratifying about the contact that fly tackle provides with the business end of things. Because the line is retrieved by pulling it in with the hand, rather than cranking it in through a train of cogs and bearings, the angler feels much closer to what is happening at the end of the line. When a fish is hooked, the feeling of direct contact is far greater than when using a fixed spool reel or multiplier, and the sense of hand to hand combat cannot be exceeded by any other type of fishing tackle that I have tried.

The fact that anglers use fly rods to catch everything from trout to tarpon underlines the aesthetic advantage which fly fishing has over other methods. Tarpon fishing is far more suited to using fixed spool reels or multipliers, but everyone seems to want to catch one on a fly, despite the inherent limitations such as casting range and speed of retrieve. It is the enjoyment of tangling with a big fish, and the skill required to tame it with nothing more than a rod and a simple drum reel that makes fly fishing the first choice for more and more of us anglers. No mechanical gadgetry or high-tech assistance required, thank you; just the angler and the fish, fighting it out. This is the beauty of fly fishing.

The appeal of bigger fish
The ever-increasing size of trout being stocked in commercially managed waters clearly indicates that there is a great interest among fly fishers in catching large fish. But big trout don't come cheap, and there are still relatively few six pounders caught each season by the average angler. On the other hand, there are many pike well in excess of six pounds in our rivers and lakes, and these can be caught at a fraction of the cost of trout fishing. The thrill of struggling with a big pike on fly tackle is something to be experienced, and one is far more likely to hook into a twenty pound pike than a twenty pound trout or salmon!

Learn it!
I have already stated that this book will provide a new and exciting alternative for the established fly fisherman, and any who begin the pursuit of pike on the fly will not be disappointed.

However, if you are in that other category - an ardent pike fan but you don't know how to fly fish - let me say this: fly fishing is easy to learn. And fly fishing for pike is much easier to learn than fly fishing for trout! I would advise you, persuade you, argue with you - and even twist your arm behind your back - to take it up. It's not expensive, nor is it difficult: it just requires a bit of practice. Make the decision now to go for it! I've dedicated the whole of the next chapter to help you get started.

If you learn to cast a fly, I assure you that you'll not regret it. In fact, it may very well become your favourite method of catching pike. And then, of course, once you've mastered pike, there's trout, and salmon, and grayling, and pollack, and bass . . .

CHAPTER 3

TACKLE

One of the most appealing aspects of fly fishing is that it requires very little tackle. I'm well used to this freedom from clutter, and I have often wondered how I'd cope if I ever took up match fishing! Every May, my home town of Enniskillen hosts one of the richest and most prestigious fishing competitions on the match angler's calendar, and hundreds of fishermen trundle in from Britain and the Continent laden down with enormous quantities of tackle. They spend half an hour setting everything up (after having made a dozen trips to the car to ferry it all down to the swim), and at the end of the day the whole process must be reversed. I think match anglers love fishing tackle as much as fishing!

Fly fishing is the antithesis of match fishing in the respect that there is little else to carry beyond a rod, a reel and a box of flies - or at least that's the way it should be. Over the years I have noticed fly fishermen gradually become more and more laden down with bits and pieces that they 'need' to go out and catch trout. I suppose this just goes to prove that much of the fishing tackle on sale today is far better at catching fishermen than fish. (Come to think of it, this penchant for tackle might have something to do with the fact that lots of match men have taken up fly fishing in recent years. Maybe the habit has been imported!)

All the bits and pieces you'll need to fly fish for pike will fit into a pocket or two of your coat, and you don't even need to carry a net. Travelling light affords complete freedom to wander from swim to swim, or even lake to lake. I have often fished two or three waters in an afternoon, or walked a few miles along a shoreline without realising how far I had gone.

Let all tackle lovers be warned - once you get used to this freedom to wander as you fish, you may not want to be tied again to a ton and a half of tackle and accessories!

The rod
Before you rush out and buy your new tackle, remember this: the law of diminishing returns applies to fishing tackle like no other commodity. A fly rod costing thirty pounds will do just about everything for the average angler that a rod ten times that price will do. Fly fishing for pike involves casting a large fly, and very little subtlety or finesse is involved, so there is no real advantage in laying out lots of money for expensive tackle. I have already pointed out that fly tackle is simple, and expensive gear will not improve your prospects. It will just give you more to worry about when you are scrambling through a hedge!

In fly fishing, the line is cast, not the fly, and all fly rods are rated according to their casting ability. This rating is usually between 4 and 10, with four being very light and ten very heavy. All makes of fly line are rated according to a universally recognised scale, so that rods and lines from different manufacturers can be suitably matched. The rating number on both rods and lines is usually preceded by the letters AFTM, which stands for The Association of Fishing Tackle Manufacturers.

Fly fishing for pike requires rods rated between AFTM 7 and 10. Lighter rods of 5-6 may be used but these can struggle to cope with the large flies which must be cast. (In fly fishing, casting becomes more difficult as the fly becomes heavier, rather than easier, as some might expect.)

I would advise a rod of not less than nine feet, and not more than ten. Casting experts say that nine to nine and a half feet is the optimum length for distance casting. Ideally it should be rated AFTM 8-9.

The reel
Again, there is no significant advantage in spending lots of

money on a fly reel. There are numerous fly reels between twenty and forty pounds in price which are perfectly suitable. Choose a reel designed for reservoir trout fishing as these hold slightly more line than standard trout fly reels. Leeda have by far the best range for both quality and price, and the Rimfly is first choice, followed by the more expensive (but lighter) LC range. These reels are extremely simple in their design, with nothing more than a click mechanism and a removable drum. The drum has an exposed flange, or rim, for slowing down a running fish with finger pressure.

The next step up is a fly reel with a disc drag. This will apply drag to the spool according to the setting, which may be varied while playing a fish. In my opinion, it is not necessary to purchase a reel with a disc drag, though such a reel may be advantageous in some circumstances. A pike which runs for twenty yards will tire itself out, even when there is no pressure exerted on it by the angler, and it is rare indeed for a pike to take more than thirty yards of line in one run. Pike are sprinters, not long distance athletes, and there will be no threat of losing your prize through not having a disc drag on your reel. All you need is a decent reserve of backing. *(Apart from all these reasons, I would still choose the simpler reel in preference to a disc drag reel. Why? For the reason stated in the last chapter - the simpler the better! I'd rather slow down a running fish with hand pressure than employ a mechanical gadget to do it for me.)*

Whichever reel you choose, remember to grease the main spindle every few years. It is not a pleasant experience to find that your 'dried out' reel seizes up the moment a good fish puts a strain on it! It happened to me once, and it certainly won't happen again!

Fly lines
Essentially, all fly lines can be divided into two categories: full fly lines and shooting heads.

Traditionally, full fly lines are about thirty yards long, and are thickly coated with a PVC type material, which varies in density to either float or sink. This line is attached to braided or monofilament backing, which only sees the light of day when a really large fish is hooked, because the average trout angler cannot cast more than thirty yards of line. This is the main drawback with standard fly lines, and is the primary reason for the development of shooting heads.

Shooting heads are only about ten yards long, but can be cast much further than full lines. They also require a lot less effort. The shooting head is attached to a special lightweight backing, and both are stripped off the reel before casting commences. The shooting head is cast as normal, except that on the final forward throw it acts like an arrowhead, pulling twenty or thirty yards of lightweight backing out through the rod rings before it lands on the water. Long distances can be achieved on each cast with ease, and large flies are much easier to handle. For our purposes, the shooting head is by far the better choice. Choose your shooting head to match the heaviest AFTM rating on your rod, or even a weight above that.

All fly lines are made to either sink (rated 'S'), or float ('F'), and this is our next consideration. We require the sinking type, but there is a little more to it than this, as sink rates vary enormously. Nowadays, many sinking lines are rated for speed of sinking, and this is measured in inches per second, (ips), or centimetres per second, (cps). A line which sinks at five or six ips is required, and these are often described as Ultra Fast Sink lines. Watch out, though, as sink rates of lines described in this way can still vary a lot. Also, be careful not to confuse the two ratings, especially when both are sometimes quoted in the same catalogue! For example a 6ips line is the equivalent of a 15cps line, so don't buy a 6cps line by mistake.

This line will cover most requirements, and will certainly do for now if you are starting out. The addition of a slow sinker will be beneficial if a lot of spring and summer fishing is anticipated, and a lead core if deep water is to be tackled regularly.

I recommend Mullarkey's of Burton-on-Trent for fly lines and backing. Their own brand of full lines and shooting heads are good quality and excellent value for money. (For further advice on lines and casting, refer to chapter 15, entitled 'Helpful Hints'.)

The shooting head backing
There are many different brands of shooting head backing on the market, but essentially there are only two types: monofilament (sometimes called solid monofilament) and braided monofilament.

Monofilament
Monofilament shooting head backing is, at first glance, the same as ordinary monofilament fishing line, but there are important differences. Ordinary monofilament fishing line is unsuitable for shooting head work because it is prone to tangling up during the cast. The various shooting head monofilament backings on the market are specially designed for this purpose and are much more limp than ordinary monofilament.

Braided monofilament
This is made from braiding a dozen or more fine monofilament strands into one hollow line, which is both lightweight and limp. Braided monofilament line will behave differently to solid monofilament during use, and both types have their own strengths and weaknesses. The jury is still out, as far as I am concerned, as to which is better.

The main advantage of solid monofilament is that it will shoot better than braided mono. The trade-off is that it needs to be stretched each time it is stripped off the reel to eliminate the coils, and it is rather more prone to serious tangles. Another disadvantage is that it will stretch much more than braided line, and bitter experience has taught me that it is difficult to set a big hook at thirty yards with stretchy line! Solid mono is not suitable for use with a standard line tray, either, whereas braided line is okay. The solid mono is also more susceptible to damage than the braided stuff.

On paper, the advantage seems to be with the braided line, but I do like to get those extra few yards on the cast! My advice is to start with the braided line, and once you become familiar with using a shooting head, try out the mono.

Advice on purchasing

With regard to braided monofilament, I do not think there is any significant difference between the various brands on the market.

However, this is not the case with solid monofilament lines. Monofilament shooting head backing is available with a flat (or oval) cross section, as well as in the standard circular cross section. I always avoid flat or oval monofilament backing because it suffers excessive wear and tear from kinks, and it can be very difficult to untangle if a snarl-up occurs.

There is also a considerable difference in quality between the different brands of circular cross section lines. I have tried most of them and the only one I would recommend is Amnesia, which is available in 20lb and 30lb breaking strains. Always choose the heavier version as it is less prone to stretching and damage.

Most shooting head backing comes on spools of around seventy yards, even though only thirty five yards are needed. I always divide the spool in half and keep one length as a spare.

Standard Backing

The shooting head backing, along with the shooting head itself, will not be enough to fill the reel spool, even if all seventy odd

yards of shooting head backing are used. Any standard monofilament line of twenty pounds or more can be used to take up the
extra capacity of the reel. Of course, it will also come in handy
if you hook a forty pounder, so take care to tie the knots carefully! (*It is important to fill the reel spool because a half-filled spool
will take ages to wind in. It will also store the casting line in smaller
loops, which are more likely to tangle.*)

Fixtures and fittings
The backing line can be attached to the shooting head backing
with a simple blood knot. The shooting head itself can be
attached to the shooting head backing by means of a braided
loop. Braided loops can be purchased from most tackle shops,
either ready made or in a DIY kit. It is important that this joint
be kept as slim as possible, because it passes through the rod
rings on each cast, and braided loops are the best compromise
between slimness and user-friendliness. Some shooting heads
come with this loop already attached, and both solid mono and
braided mono can be attached to the loop with a half blood
knot.

Another braided loop is permanently attached at the business
end of the shooting head, and the final length of fishing line is
tied on here, with the fly on the other end. This is called the
'leader', or 'cast', and is usually two metres in length.

The whole set-up may sound complex when described on
paper, but it is actually very simple. The two set-ups are
summarised below in order of attachment to the reel.

REEL - ORDINARY BACKING - SHOOTING HEAD BACKING -
SHOOTING HEAD - LEADER

REEL - ORDINARY BACKING - FULL FLY LINE - LEADER

If you are starting out from scratch and don't want to be

bothered with all this, I suggest buying the goods from a tackle dealer who will agree to load the lines onto the reel for you.

The trace

A trace is not required for trout fishing because ordinary mono can easily cope with their teeth. Pike, on the other hand, have lots of pin-sharp teeth, which will slice through light nylon with ease, so a strong trace of at least 30 cms in length must be attached between the end of the leader and the fly to prevent this happening.

Two different kinds of trace may be used: wire, or very thick nylon monofilament. The traditional pike trace is a length of wire, which is impervious to the pike's teeth, and is the only truly fail-safe material. The trouble is, wire traces are not at all suited to fly fishing. Wire is heavy, highly visible and prone to kinking. Flies need to be changed regularly and it is not easy to attach a fly to a length of wire neatly and quickly.

I almost always use heavy monofilament in preference to wire, as it is much more user friendly. However, it must be said that there is a great variation in the performance of different types of nylon monofilament in resisting the pike's teeth, and this topic is discussed in detail in chapter 15 under the section entitled 'Snap-offs and monofilament traces'.

The best monofilament material I have used to date is Climax Saltwater Tippet, in 50lb breaking strain. It costs around £3 for a ten metre spool, and is available from Tidelines in central London. I never use any other make as Climax is considerably better than anything I have tried so far.

When using monofilament traces, it is absolutely essential to check the line nearest to the fly after every strike. Cut off any line which has been chafed by the pike's teeth and re-tie the fly. My leaders are usually somewhere between four and eight feet in length, with about half made of 12lb monofilament and half of Climax. I join these two lengths with a two turn surgeon's knot. The hard monofilament is tied directly on to the fly using a three turn half blood knot, while the light end of the leader is tied to the braided loop on the shooting head with a five or six turn half blood.

If I am in with a chance of a really big fish, I will sometimes use wire, though I must confess to using it less and less with each passing season. For example, I fish for both trout and pike on Lough Sheelin, where fly-caught trout average somewhere around three pounds, and many 30lb pike have been taken. (Only recently an angler hooked and landed a 32lb pike on a trout fly while fishing in a competition.) I'd never forgive myself if I hooked the fish of a lifetime and it sawed through my thick mono leader during a prolonged fight! Having said that, my confidence in monofilament traces has been boosted greatly by using Climax for the past two seasons.

Casting a shooting head

For those fly fishers who have never used a shooting head, I offer some advice in chapter 15.

Learning to cast

There are many books available on how to cast a fly, and it is not the purpose of this book to cover that topic. A quick visit to your local library will do the trick!

It is worth pointing out here that most casting books will advise learning to cast with a full line before trying a shooting head, but I can see no reason why one shouldn't begin with a shooting head. Learning to cast a fly line is all about timing, and once this has been learned, it is as easy to adapt from a shooting head to a standard line as it is to do things the other way round.

CHAPTER 4

REQUIREMENTS FOR SUCCESS WITH BIGGER PIKE

When pike are feeding, they are not too difficult to catch. Many superb bags have been recorded on days when the fry are shoaled up against the shore, and attack after attack sends little fish jumping in all directions. It's spectacular and exciting stuff!
However, it is rare to find pike in this sort of feeding frenzy. For much of the time, they lie on the bottom, or near the shoreline along weed margins, waiting for an opportune meal to swim by. Often, a pike will not even attempt to attack a catchable fish if it requires any more than a moderate effort. When pike are in this mood, (which seems to be fairly often, especially for the bigger fish), they are difficult to catch, but it is still possible to persuade them. Despite these regular bouts of lethargy, there are very few pike, I think, that will ignore a tempting offering which is twitched slowly past the nose.

This means that the operative words for many pike fishing situations are 'deep' and 'slow'. The problem is that most pike lures are not presented in this way. Usually, a spoon or spinner is drawn fairly quickly through the water in an attempt to induce an instinctive strike - or simply to avoid catching the bottom. Although there is no doubt that fishing deep and slow will produce more big fish, actually doing it is much easier said that done, because such an approach throws up several problems all at once. If the offering is to be 'twitched slowly past the pike's nose' the fish has lots of time to inspect the lure. The lure must be life-like enough to fool a pike into taking it for a meal, even after a good look at close range. The other problem is how to fish consistently close to the bottom without snagging up. Big pike lie right on the bottom most of the time, and if a fish is not inclined to feed, there is not much use in presenting the bait several yards above her head.

It is here that we begin to see the inherent limitations of spinning or plug fishing. It is virtually impossible to fish a spoon bait consistently near the bottom without endless snags and lost tackle. If the pike are not in the mood to strike at a briskly retrieved lure, slowing down the retrieve will encourage snags as well as giving the fish more time to reject the bait. Undoubtedly, a plug will fool pike more efficiently than a spoon bait on those days when a slow retrieve is needed, but the problem of fishing it close to the bottom without snagging remains. Many anglers resort to dead baiting as the only reliable way of getting down and staying down to catch the larger specimens.

Success at last!
For years I ran hot and cold on the problem of how to take large pike on the fly. Sure, when the fish are lying in shallow water they can be taken on big flies, and of course small pike can be caught in the shallows all year round. For the most part, though, larger pike doggedly lie on the bottom in deeper water, and consistently persuading them to take a fly is no easy matter. One must be able to fish dead slow in order to increase the chances of tempting the bigger fish; the lure must be able to hug the bottom for good presentation and yet avoid snags; and finally, it must be realistic enough to fool an experienced pike into taking it for a fish.

After endless attempts to find a successful tactic, I eventually hit upon a winning formula. I was seized with the inspiration one day as I glanced through a fly fishing magazine at the newsagents. Three or four components came together all at once and suddenly I realised how to approach the problem. A certain type of fly, combined with an unusual approach and if I could just meet all the requirements for the fly, well . . .

I raced home to see if I could produce my idea at the vice, and after a bit of experimentation, I had an impressive looking result. About a week later, I paid a visit to an old friend, Ballydoolagh Lough, where I had lost umpteen spoon baits as a schoolboy. It was the end of January, and there was no trout fishing to keep me occupied, so I was happy just to put up my rod for the first time that year, even if it was only to wet a line. I was a lot happier when, an hour later, I had two pike of four and six pounds, both taken in about fifteen feet of water!

I was excited at my new discovery, and everywhere I tried the method it seemed to produce fish. I have hardly used any other technique for pike since, and I rarely blank when I go pike fishing. In fact, this method has been entirely responsible for resurrecting my interest in the species.

In the next chapter I will outline this simple and very effective approach.

CHAPTER 5

The Magic Method

Like most other useful developments, there is no spectacular invention or discovery involved in this technique - it is simply an effective adaptation of an existing fly fishing method.

Years ago I was a member of a fly fishing club based at the Queen Mother Reservoir in Dachet, West London. The reservoir is a concrete bowl three and a third miles in circumference with very deep water throughout. The trout foisted a lot of attention on the huge shoals of sticklebacks which hugged the bottom right down to forty or more feet. Initially, fast sink lines were used to get down to them, but it was very difficult to present a fly near the bottom without picking up all sorts of debris.

It didn't take long before the anglers devised an ingenious method for catching these bottom feeders. The answer was to use a buoyant fly in combination with a fast sink line. The fly was small enough to be pulled down by the fast sink line, but it would sit up off the bottom once all the line had touched down. A five foot leader, for example, would leave the fly suspended about five feet clear of the bottom. A gentle draw on the line would cause the fly to dive and at the same time move laterally. A slow and constant retrieve would cause the fly to swim about two feet above bottom. Stopping would allow it to float up to its maximum clearance of five feet, and a faster retrieve would cause it to fish closer to the bottom. In this way, it was possible to fish as slow a retrieve as you liked, with the fly constantly fishing no more than a few feet off the bottom.

The first flies were called boobies and razzlers, and these were perfected by anglers such as Micky Bewick at the club. The boobies were tied with polystyrene eyes fixed onto the hook using ladies stockings, and the razzlers used plastazote. These buoyant flies accounted for many large rainbows and the popularity of this method has spread far and wide in trout fishing circles since then. *(By way of record, it seems the idea of combining a buoyant fly with a sunk line did not originate at the Queen Mother Reservoir. Conventional opinion credits the late Richard Walker with the innovation, who called his buoyant pattern Rasputin. His habit, apparently, was to tie it on a short leader during lunch and throw the whole lot out and let the suspended fry imitation fish completely static.)*

Boobies and razzlers are far too small to seriously interest pike, and it was only the combination of this method with a new pattern of fly which completed the picture, and provided the key to consistently taking large pike on fly tackle - a goal which I had so long pursued.

CHAPTER 6

THE BALLYDOOLAGH BOMBER

I have christened this fly the Ballydoolagh Bomber, (pronounced Bally-doola), as it went down a bomb on my first trip to Ballydoolagh! (Quite a tongue twister, you'll agree, especially if you're not Irish!)

The criteria which this fly must meet, if it is to succeed, are many. First, it must be fairly large if it is to consistently take big pike. Second, it has to be buoyant. Third, it must be light if it is to be cast any distance with fly rod and line. Fourth, it must not have a bulky profile, which seriously inhibits casting range. Fifth, it must be lifelike enough to fool pike, especially when fished slowly.

It's a tall order, but all these requirements are met by the Ballydoolagh Bomber.

The Ballydoolagh Bomber

Hook: 4/0 sea hook.
Head: white plastazote.
Body: various colours of long fibre bucktail.
Gill hackle: red cock hackle.

The hook. I use the Mustad Nordic bend, pattern no. 4447B, size 4/0. Originally I used salmon irons, but these tended to rust quicker. I also think that sea hooks retain a better point over time, and I have found out the hard way that sharp hook points are very important in pike fishing, especially when you only have one!

The head. The plastazote head is the key to the success of the

Ballydoolagh Bomber. It provides several vital ingredients all at once. It not only supplies the required buoyancy, but does so in such a way that causes the fly to swim upright at all times. Adding buoyancy to a fly can leave it very bulky and difficult to cast, but the head of this fly is remarkably aerodynamic, and does not seriously impede casting. It also provides a very life-like appearance and an ideal shape and surface for painting in eyes and other fishy features. Because the buoyancy is at the front of the fly, the Ballydoolagh Bomber will sit near to horizontal when static, due to the balancing effect of the sunk line pulling downwards on the eye of the hook against the buoyant head. This helps to mimic the attitude of a food fish during a slow retrieve.

Plastazote can be bought from any good fly tying supplier. (It also has many non-fishing applications, such as swimming floats or flip flops.) The best colours for heads are light grey and white.

The body. The body of the fly is tied with extra-long bucktail fibres. Bucktail is quite stiff, but when long fibres are used, the slightest movement causes a very life-like 'pulse' to travel along the length of the body. The action of drawing the fly through water causes the bucktail to cling together into a fish-shaped body.

It is worth noting that bucktail varies quite a lot, depending on the supplier. Some pieces have fibres that are nearly twice as long as others. The longer fibres are straighter, and are undoubtedly better than the shorter fibres, especially for the largest flies. It is well worth specifying this when purchasing, as long fibre bucktail will considerably improve the end product. It is also worth noting that bucktail varies consider-ably in the thickness of the fibres, and this makes an enormous difference to the action of the fly in the water. The best type is the finer hair, which usually has a slight crinkle in it, whereas the thicker fibres are straight.

I have also experimented with softer hair, such as goat. This is more flexible than bucktail, and will produce a more pronounced 'wiggle', but it is too soft and fine for such a large fly. It tends to cling together tightly when wet and this deadens the action and also makes the fly heavier by holding water during the cast.

Finally, the red hackle, placed between the head and the body, is ideally located to imitate the red gills which often become visible in an injured or struggling fish. This is an important 'trigger' for pike to attack.

Other requirements

You will need super glue and a sharp knife. I find the retractable knives that have snap-off sections to be most suitable for the job in hand. Extra strong thread is also essential.

Tying the Ballydoolagh Bomber

The first job is to make the head. Cut a 10mm thick strip of plastazote off the end of the block, using a suitable straight edge. Trim it so that the final piece is about 20 mm wide and 10mm thick. (My own plastazote blocks are 18mm deep so I just cut a 10mm slice off each end - like cutting a loaf of bread.) This strip is then cut across diagonally to form the basic shape of a Ballydoolagh Bomber head, as shown below. The long side should be about 18-20mm and the short side about 5mm.

Take your dubbing needle and thrust it through the foam at the point where you want the hook shank to enter and exit, as shown above. The best point is right in the middle of the nose. Take care to keep the needle vertical as it is inserted. I often use a compass in preference to my dubbing needle as the wire is thicker, and this permits easier fitting on to the hook.

Carefully slide the foam over the eye of the hook, using the hole as a guide. (Make sure the head ends up the right way round on the shank - with the nose forward.) Lay a coat of superglue along the shank just behind the eye and draw the plastazote into position, drawing it up so that it is touching the eye of the hook. A drop of glue at either end assists in fixing the material permanently. Fix the head in an upright position, with most of the foam head above the shank rather than below, as this encourages the fly to swim in an upright attitude. The head can be shaped with scissors when the glue has set.

The easiest way to shape the head is to make four cuts from the nose towards the back of the head, cutting off the four corners. Hold the scissors close to the hook eye to start each cut, leaving a pointed nose. Take less foam off as you cut towards the back of the head. This will provide the basic shape, which can be trimmed until an even finish is achieved.

1. *Carefully insert a needle through foam head. I often use a compass in preference to a dubbing needle because the wire is thicker. This makes is easier to mount on to the hook.*

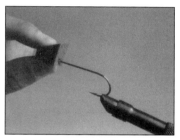

2. *Gently work the head over the eye of the hook.*

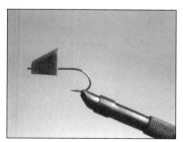

3. *Use superglue to fix in position. Note that most of the foam is above the hook shank, which causes the fly to swim in an upright attitude.*

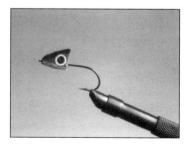

4. *The head is shaped with scissors and painted.*

Once the head is in place, the next step is to tie in the bucktail body. All fish have the lightest colours on their bellies, gradually getting darker towards the top. This is a general rule for tying fry or fish patterns, and should always be heeded. I usually tie white in at the bottom, the lightest tones next, and finish off at the top with the darkest colours.

The bucktail will fish best if tied in correctly and the general aim is to persuade it to sit out from the hook shank. This gives a life-like swimming action as the Ballydoolagh Bomber is drawn through the water, and it makes a significant difference to the success of the fly.

Lay a tight bed of thread over the shank and varnish, as this will help prevent the whole tying from turning on the shank. Begin by tying in the lightest coloured bucktail towards the back of the hook shank. Use a strong thread and pull this as tight as you dare after each turn. This will cause the bucktail to spin around the shank and flare out. Varnish the butt ends of the fibres and tie these down tight to the shank, moving towards the eye. Do not tie them in along the full length of the shank. Once secured, trim off the excess butts to leave space on the shank for the final bunch of bucktail.

The second bunch is placed on top of the first, and tied in. Do not let this bunch (or any subsequent bunches) spin on the shank, but keep it on top.

 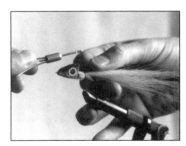

1. Offer up a fairly large bunch of bucktail.
This forms the main part of the body.

2. Bind the bucktail down tightly,
spinning it on the shank.

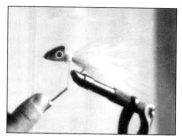

3. A drop of varnish will secure fibres in place, as well as softening them to assist splaying

4. Offer up a smaller bunch of darker bucktail to form the back.

5. Do not allow this bunch to spin around the shank.

6. Whip finish, and change to fine thread for the gill hackle.

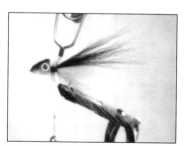

7. Tie in and wind a red cock hackle. Finally, tie off behind the head and varnish.

The final bunch is tied in forward of the first two bunches, right behind the foam head and on top of the hook shank. This should be the darkest colour. Whip backwards towards the bend to the spot where the first two bunches finish. Tying up fairly tight to this will cause the fibres to sit up nicely against the butts of the first bunches. Remember to prevent the bucktail spinning on the hook shank.

I usually tie in two or three colours, but more may be used according to preference. Several contrasting colours may be used, or various shades of the same colour, but always remember to get darker towards the top. It is also important to avoid tying in too much bucktail. Too much body material will impair the effectiveness of the fly in several ways. As well as adding weight to the fly, densely packed hair tends to retain more water during casting, thus adding even more weight. It also deadens the action of the fly in the water without making it any larger. A fairly sparse dressing is best.

The tying is completed by winding a red cock hackle just behind the head. There will be quite a thick bed of tied-in bucktail here, and the hackle is simply wound on top of it. Tie off between the hackle and the back of the head with a whip finish or a knot.

Painting the head

Black and white varnish or enamel paint can be used to paint the head. Follow the simple rule of dark at the top and light at the bottom. An eye on each side completes the job. The easiest way to paint in eyes is to cut the point off a sharpened pencil, about half way up the exposed wood. Cut it off square to make a small circle and dip this in the paint and press it onto the plastazote. This is much quicker than trying to paint in a perfectly round eye. To make the best eyes, make a larger white circle first and then put a smaller black circle in the centre when it is dry. The eye is probably the most important trigger of all for the pike, so it is worthwhile, especially for slowly retrieved flies.

CHAPTER 8

General Tactics

Like most art forms, fishing is full of contradictions. Many anglers develop their thinking and approach along different lines, and, contrary to all logic, often arrive at completely opposing viewpoints. I have met trout anglers who concentrate much of their effort on getting the colour of the fly just right, while others swear that colour has little or nothing to do with it - presentation and size are the important issues. I'm sure that many anglers who fish with the Ballydoolagh Bomber will develop their own theories and favoured approaches, and these may well vary from my own. However, I will outline in this chapter what I consider to be the most successful approaches for me, on the waters I fish.

Fishing the water

As you will have gathered by now, I love the freedom to wander as I fish. Nice though it may be, there is a purpose in it too. If I cast twice into the same spot and spend five minutes working my fly through it without a result, the chances are that I will not have any joy on the third cast. It is much more profitable to cast into unfished water than to cover the old ground over and over again.

If I approach a section of bank, I will usually start at one end so I can work my way along it methodically. I always cover the water close in before I wade out and disturb the margins. This habit bore fruit only recently when my wife had to visit a nearby town for a few hours. She dropped me off on the way at a 'new' lake which I had spotted on a map, but when I arrived at the water's edge, it was virtually unfishable due to tall reeds. There was only one break in the reeds through which I could gain access to the water, and I had two hours to kill before my wife came back for me! Normally I would have run the fly through this long, shallow opening a few times before wading out, but in this case I took extra time to cover it carefully, casting right up to the weed margin and teasing the fly home just under the surface in three feet of water. I was rewarded with a very fit pike which gave me a full ten minute battle, interspersed with several spectacular leaps! I didn't get to weigh her, but she was the only good fish I caught there, and I hooked the fish at the very spot where I chose to stand for the remaining hour to cover the water beyond the reeds.

I normally adopt a fan casting approach, beginning with a cast along the shore in the shallower water. I then cast all the way around in an arc until I am casting along the shore in the other direction. I then walk along the bank about thirty yards and repeat the process. When I hit a good fish, I hang around a little longer in that spot.

Favourite retrieves

My most commonly used retrieve is the 'Tease Retrieve'. The overall pace is very slow, and it is a combination of static pauses, very slow draws, twitches, and the odd sudden, swift pull. I usually have to remind myself to slow down, and I have taken many fish during the pause when the fly sits static, or is slowly rising up in the water. These takes never ceases to amaze me, especially as the fish has lots of time to inspect the fly at close quarters. Maybe it is a testimony to the imitative qualities of the fly, or maybe the pike just loves an easy target. I don't really know, except that it works.

I sometimes use a 'Fast-Fast-Stop' retrieve to take advantage of the pike's weakness for sudden changes of tempo. A pike's attention will often be caught by swift movement, so I make two short, fast pulls on the fly before leaving it to settle into a static pose. Instead of taking it, a pike will sometimes eye up a static fly with curiosity, but if it suddenly twitches, or moves off, the pike will lunge at it.

The 'Float and Dive' approach is a further development of this, and is one of the best ways to get your fly noticed across a wider area, especially if the water is clear. In effect, it is the 'sink and draw' method in reverse. Choose a fairly buoyant fly and use it with a longer than normal leader of about eight feet. The method involves a moderately swift retrieve - not too fast - of three or four yards at a time, followed by a pause of ten to fifteen seconds. During the pause the fly will rise up high in the water, and the next retrieve will cause it to dive forwards and down towards the bottom again. It will then slowly rise up in the water until the next retrieve. The great advantage of this method is that a fly which is five or six feet clear of the bottom will be much more visible than one which hugs the bottom. As the fly swims up from the bottom during the pause, it acts like a beacon to any pike in the vicinity before diving back for cover, simulating an injured fish. A pike will often hit the fly during the pause, and concentration is needed if these static takes are to be detected. I watch carefully for a backwards movement in the line, or sometimes I feel a tug. Watching the line is more reliable than feel, so constant attention is required, but either way it is easy to miss these takes.

Clearly, the potential for developing new retrieve patterns is great, and over time many anglers will develop and refine new and effective methods for persuading the pike.

Varying the leader length
The distance off the lake bed at which the fly is fished can be critical to success. This distance is primarily determined by the speed of the retrieve, (assuming, of course, that the fly line is on the bottom to start with). A briskly retrieved fly will fish very near the bottom regardless of leader length, but the length becomes more important as the retrieve slows down. A slow

retrieve and a seven foot leader may mean that you are fishing anywhere from three to five feet off the bottom, depending on the buoyancy of the fly, the density of the fly line, and the speed of the retrieve.

In winter, for example, when pike are likely to be dour, it may be necessary to fish a very slow retrieve only a foot or two off the bottom, and shortening the leader is the only way to achieve this. Leader length can go right down to as little as three feet in these circumstances.

It is worth noting here that a five foot leader does not actually suspend the fly five feet off the bottom. The buoyant fly may lift a few feet of fly line off the bottom before it hits equilibrium, leaving it six feet or more above the deck. In practice, though, the fly will take a long time to reach equilibrium, and a five foot leader with a slow retrieve may only fish the fly at an average of about three feet off the bottom. It is clear from this that varying the buoyancy of the fly will alter its action and depth in the water.

It is also worth remembering to avoid fast, long pulls in quick succession in snaggy areas, as this action will bring the fly right down to the bottom and may result in the loss of the fly. When there is a threat of snagging up, the best insurance is to slow the retrieve right down.

Fishing weeded up water

In summer, lake beds often become overgrown with weed, restricting most kinds of lure fishing to the surface layers. It is possible, however, even in this difficult environment, to fish the Ballydoolagh Bomber and sinking line in the conventional manner. Certain types of weed will support the line so one can simply allow the line to settle on it as though it were the bottom. Big pike will often choose to lie over a weed bed as their camouflage is designed for just such an environment, so taking the trouble to fish in these waters is well worth while.

There are a few things worth noting when fishing over a bed of weed. Firstly, you cannot avoid getting snagged up in the weed from time to time. However, there are several steps you can take to minimise these frustrating occurrences. The most important is to always maintain a very slow retrieve, which will keep the fly higher up off the bottom. It is also helpful to use a more buoyant fly. This assists in keeping the leader more upright, which helps it to cut through the weed, and is more effective than increasing the length of the leader with a less buoyant fly. A weed guard is just about essential in these conditions. (See chapter entitled 'Helpful Hints' for tying instructions.)

Although fishing weeded up water in summer with the conventional approach can be productive, there is a far more interesting and sporting approach, which we will discuss in the next chapter.

Spooked fish

If you spend time wading or rowing in weedy, shallow water, sooner or later you will spook a fish. Its presence will be betrayed by a boil, sometimes followed by a bow wave if the water is very shallow. Always try to see which way the fish went, because these fish are well worth casting to. Spooked pike will usually only swim ten or twenty yards before stopping, and will readily attack a bait, even as they are fleeing.

My trout fishing partner, Gary Montgomery, witnessed this to his astonishment one sunny day which we wasted in the fruit-less pursuit of trout on L. Mask. When the evening rise failed to materialise, I persuaded him to row me round Cushlough bay to see if I could get a pike. As we rowed over shallow weed a large swirl betrayed a pike, and the bow wave clearly indicated which way the fish went. I shouted "Watch this!" as I cast beyond the fish, and a second later the flat water erupted as the pike slammed the fly and came off. Gary was astonished! He was speechless when I hooked the 6lb fish on the next cast. Pike are certainly not like trout!

If you see which way the fish heads when it is spooked, cast beyond it and retrieve briskly. Expect a spectacular hit. If you don't know which way it went, try fan casting, because the likelihood is that the fish is not far away. It is surprising just how many of these fish will take the fly.

I remember reading somewhere that Scottish landowners of old used this tactic to assist them in catching pike. Apparently, they were rowed along the shore of a lake as the servants beat around in the shallows to drive the pike out towards their master.

Dealing with playful pike

When the pike are in a fickle mood it can be frustratingly difficult to tempt them. On some days it seems as though every pike in the area will chase and nip the fly, but none will go for a positive take. Early one morning I fished a shoreline for an hour and had five offers, but no fish. I tried everything - fast, slow, static - the lot, but I couldn't hook a fish.

It is well known that trout will sometimes nip the tail of a fly, and pike will do the same. I first experienced this while fishing a clean bottom along a weed margin when I felt a little pluck. Now, in trout fishing it can sometimes be difficult to distinguish between a pluck from a fish and catching up in soft weed, but I did not expect any gentle takes from pike! In my book, they always clamped their mouths tightly over the fly producing a solid thump, so my habit was to ignore such plucks as being weed. But on this occasion I knew the bottom was clean, so I deliberately pulled a long brisk draw on the line and was immediately rewarded with a positive strike. The fish had nipped my slow-moving fly, and when the fly fled in response, the pike charged after it and took! I am certain that had I continued my slow retrieve, the fish would not have touched it again. The response of a real fish would be to flee, so speeding up the retrieve when a pike nips the fly would seem to be the best approach when this happens. I have successfully used this tactic many times since to produce a more positive take second time around.

It does not guarantee success, though. Some pike will resolutely refuse to open their mouths and engulf the fly, yet they will chase and generally act in a way that gets the angler all het up! Such fish are best forgotten because if they don't take on the first few casts, they are unlikely to be tempted no matter how long you stay there. I wasted an hour once chasing just such a fish. My first cast landed six feet from a clump of weeds, and before the fly was dragged under by the sinking line, a pike went for it. She jumped completely out of the water, but missed the static fly by about two feet. When a big pike wants to grab something, she doesn't miss it by two feet, so I should have read the signs at the start. This fish wanted to play, not eat. Four more times she followed my fly all the way to the bank, turning away with a flash and a boil at the last second. I threw everything at it - fast retrieves, slow retrieves, static, bright flies, dark flies, smaller flies, the lot. I even went back there that afternoon and spent another fifteen minutes, this time without any show. I'd have spent my time better by moving on and fishing new water.

Dealing with genuine misses

On other occasions, the pike will genuinely miss the fly. Of course, this is only noticeable in surface fishing, where the fly is visible throughout the retrieve, and the pike can sometimes be seen coming for the fly before the actual take. I never cease to be amazed at how often a pike will explode out of the water at the fly, only to miss it cleanly, or just graze it. When this happens, the instinctive reaction is to lift the rod in a strike, but this must be resisted as it only accelerates the fly away from the area. I have found that most of these fish will attack the fly a second time once they re-locate it, and the best option is to continue with a very slow retrieve after the first attempt. It will often take five or more seconds before the pike makes a second attempt, which is usually successful. If the pike doesn't strike again, always wait for a few seconds and cast to the spot a second time.

Most of these misses seem to be genuine rather than playful, because so many of the fish will hammer the fly when given a second chance. I have often wondered if the pike's ability to measure a surface target properly is somehow impaired by the reflection or the disturbance caused by the fly at the surface. The failure usually occurs with smaller pike, and I think it is due to inexperience at hitting a surface target.

Finally, I will offer that well worn but much ignored advice: Always leave your fly to sit for a second or two in the water at the end of each cast. In trout fishing this is day one stuff, yet there is hardly an angler in the business who has not pulled the fly right out of a trout's mouth at the end of the cast, only to be left staring at the boil on the water where the fish turned away in haste. It is well recognised in trout fishing that lifting a deeply fished fly up through the water and stopping it just under the surface at the end of a retrieve will often cause a fish to race up and grab it. It is known as 'hanging the fly', and pike respond to it equally well. As your fly comes up towards the top, a pike which has been following it will sometimes charge after it at the last second. Learning to pause right at the end of the retrieve will certainly produce fish which would have otherwise been missed.

Hooks

Undoubtedly, the fact that there is only one hook will also contribute to missed takes. Some people have suggested tying Ballydoolagh Bombers with small trailing trebles, but I am loath to do so. For most of my fishing career I have been used to hooking fish with single irons, and these inflict far less damage than trebles. Several times I have fly fished with a friend who used a plug or a spoon, and I have been quite shocked at the extent of the damage which trebles inflict on pike, especially when more than one treble is used. Last season I spent quite a bit of time on a water that was heavily fished with lures and livebaits, and I was appalled at the number of fish I caught with serious injuries, especially to the jaws and teeth. One poorly-conditioned twelve pounder I caught had one of its gills torn out at the back, and it was hanging out through the gill opening. These injuries are much worse, I think, when both the top and bottom jaws have been hooked by the same treble. It is very difficult to extract such a hook without using considerable force. Single hooks inflict very little damage by comparison, and are quick and easy to extract.

In my view, this is well worth losing a few extra pike for. It also gives the pike a sporting chance of escaping, and keeps the angler on his toes right up to the last seconds of the fight. This only adds to the excitement.

Varying the buoyancy

Every fly will fish slightly differently, as no two are identical. Some will perform better than others, depending on colour, density of the body, the amount of buoyancy and the overall shape of the head. The factor which has the greatest influence on the action of the fly in the water is the amount of buoyancy, and this should be taken into account in both the speed and type of retrieve adopted with that fly.

A fly with a lot of buoyancy will not behave as naturally during a very slow retrieve as one that is closer to equilibrium. Each time you stop your retrieve, the fly will rise up sharply in the water, and settle in a 'head down' attitude, which is not conducive to fooling the pike. I normally use the most buoyant flies to fish over weed or snaggy bottoms, and I usually retrieve this fly using a series of very short jerks - a sort of mini sink and draw approach. This tends to tease the pike, or even to annoy them into a strike, and it can be very effective.

A fly will be much more buoyant than normal when freshly used from dry. After about ten minutes of use it will settle to a stable level of buoyancy. This excess buoyancy can be overcome by holding the dry fly in the water and squeezing it between finger and thumb. This will release small air bubbles from the body and head, bringing it to its normal buoyancy immediately.

The Ballydoolagh Bomber changes shape dramatically when wet.
The fish-like profile is enhanced by a lively action in the water.

Varying the colour

Changing the colour of the fly will, in my opinion, make a difference, but only on certain days. The trouble is that it's very difficult to establish whether changing to a different colour was actually responsible for catching a fish - maybe it would have been caught anyway! However, it seems there are situations where changing the colour does makes a real difference.

I once had an experience that put me off green flies for life, so terrible and unutterably traumatic was that day! After a summer thunderstorm I decided to visit my old friend

Ballydoolagh Reservoir for an evening's fishing. The lake was flat calm, and I fished a green and white Ballydoolagh Bomber on the surface. I had eight hits from pike, but only succeeded in landing one fish, and I couldn't figure out what was wrong.

My ninth fish boiled at the fly and refused it, but what a boil! I sat bolt upright, realising that this fish was big. After waiting for about a minute, I cast over the spot a second time, and stripped the fly home. A huge bow wave followed the fly all the way back, and I saw a truly enormous pike stop short of my rod tip, pause and then speed away. The outstanding impression I was left with was the size of its jaw, particularly the width from one side to the other. I'll not describe how I felt! I changed flies, lines, everything, but I didn't see the fish again. I moved on, and finished the evening using a red and white fly. By the time I got back to the car, I had successfully hooked and landed every subsequent offer! I didn't miss another fish all evening with the red fly, after missing eight out of nine with the green.

Was it a fluke? I don't know for sure, but I went off green flies in a big way! (I was even more disappointed the following Saturday morning when my friend Jonny Phenix and I caught two doubles of ten and a half and eleven and a half pounds. They looked diminutive in the water compared to the fish I had missed three days before, and underlined for me just how large the fish was.)

In choosing colours for flies, it is worth remembering that lure fishing depends entirely on visual stimulation, and the first task is to get the fly noticed. A red and white combination is hard to beat on this count. Red and white (or red and yellow) is my favourite combination, followed by black and white. I also favour a predominately white fly at dusk when the light is going, as this will be the most visible. I will always choose a red fly for fishing in cloudy water. (Red light has the longest wavelength of all the colours in the spectrum, and this maximises its visibility in difficult conditions.)

It does seem that certain colour combinations are more successful than others, but are they successful because more people use them, or do they really trigger off more strikes than other colours? My own opinion is that certain colours do attract more strikes, as witnessed by the universal popularity of black\orange, black\white and red\white combinations. It is worth noting that these are bright colours and high contrast combinations. A good source of inspiration is to flick through a tackle magazine and look at the pike lures for the best colour combinations, and try tying your flies to match.

Landing pike

I never carry a net when I am bank fishing or wading. I find it gets tangled up in everything, and landing a pike by hand is relatively easy, unlike a salmon or trout. Even when I am boat fishing, I will not usually take a net, preferring instead to land my fish by hand.

A pike can easily be landed by grasping it from the top, just behind the gills, and lifting it out of the water. Grasp it between fingers and thumb, with the thumb and forefinger nearest the head. Be careful not to squeeze too hard, as this can injure the fish; also watch out for the very delicate gills - make sure you grasp it behind the gill covers. The fish will usually keep still until you set it down, but if it does wriggle, try not to drop it! Pike up to fifteen pounds can be safely landed this way with just a little practice and a reasonably strong grip.

Much larger fish can also be landed by hand, but by a different method. The fish must be well played out before this method can be safely executed. When the fish is lying on its side, slip a finger or two under the nearest gill flap and move it round towards the chin until you can go no further. There is a thick, fleshy lump here where the two gill covers meet. Slip one of the first two fingers across the membrane which divides the two gill openings and the pike can be gripped and held here until it is lifted clear of the water and unhooked. Most, or all, of the pike's weight can be supported by this grip, but I prefer to place my free hand under the fish to spread the load, especially when lifting a large fish.

Alternatively, a very large pike can be beached. When boat fishing, I will sometimes row to the shore to beach a big fish rather than wrestle with it in the boat.

1. Played out.

2. Ready to land.

3. Take hold.

4. Lift the fish out.

Unhooking pike

This is usually an awkward process at best, and can be dangerous to the hands if care is not taken. The average pike has seven
hundred teeth, and its jaws can snap shut suddenly and power-
fully. The effect on fingers is similar to drawing a cheese grater
swiftly across the knuckles. It's not funny.

If the fish is hooked towards the front of the mouth, it can be
unhooked by inserting pointed-nosed pliers or artery forceps
into the mouth. This is not as easy as it sounds, because the fish
will most likely have its mouth clamped shut. Never try to
force the mouth open by pushing the pliers between the lips. A
pike can be persuaded to open its mouth by sliding a finger
under a gill flap and up towards the chin, where the two gill
flaps meet. A gentle pull at this point will open the mouth
every time. (Be careful, because this sometimes induces a vio-
lent wriggle.) Grip the bend of the fly with the pliers and push
it out of the fish and remove it carefully from the pike's mouth.
(Much of the damage to pike flies occurs during the unhooking
process, so taking a little extra care is well worthwhile.)

If the whole fly is inside the pike's mouth, (which is often the
case), the best access for unhooking it is through the gill flaps.
Lay the fish on its back, and straddle it, with one knee each side
of the fish, just behind the head. The fish will lie more quietly
when it is upside down, and this position will give you access
to the mouth cavity through the gill covers. Carefully lifting
each gill flap for inspection will usually reveal the hook, and it
can be gripped with pointed nose pliers or forceps and pulled
out. The pliers are inserted through the gills, and care needs to
be taken not to damage them. The fly will still be inside the
pike's mouth once unhooked, and can be removed from the
front, or through the gill openings. Open the pike's mouth
(as described above) and remove the fly carefully. This can be
awkward, as every tooth slants backwards, and the hook will do
everything in its power to catch in the fish again as you pull it

out! Do not, under any circumstances, put your fingers in the pike's mouth to lift it out: if it clamps shut and the fish wriggles, it will shred your flesh to the bone. With larger fish, it is easier to pull the fly out through the gill opening and cut it off, rather than trying to remove it via the mouth.

Some anglers still use gags to keep the mouth open. This is a device which is inserted into the pike's mouth and two spring-loaded arms force the jaws open. I am not a big fan of gags as they can apply far too much pressure on the pike's jaws, as well as damaging the tongue and the roof of the mouth. With a little care and patience, pike can be unhooked and returned without causing serious harm to either the angler or the fish.

CHAPTER 9

SURFACE AND MID-WATER FISHING

There are many significant benefits to be gained by using a buoyant fly with a sinking line. The principal one - that it can be fished consistently close to the bottom without snagging - has been discussed at length in the preceding chapters. However, there are other advantages which were not initially apparent to me when I began using this approach. The combination of a buoyant fly and a sinking line is superbly suited to surface and mid-water fishing, too, and of all the methods described in this book, surface fishing is by far my favourite, and I relish the opportunity to discuss it here!

Fishing the Surface
When conditions are right, fishing the surface will produce far more pike than any other method. Just the other week I took twenty seven from the shore of a lake in a morning, and every one took the fly right on the surface.

Surface fishing provides the angler with a wonderful visual spectacle which makes it the most thrilling of all pike fishing methods. Spending a relaxing afternoon watching your fly innocently wafting along just under the surface on a sultry summer's day may tempt your mind to wander, and the buzz of insects and the warmth of the sun might even induce sleepiness. But beware - 'Bang!' The sudden violence of a surface attack from a pike will send the heart racing! It is not uncommon to see a fish coming for the fly before it takes, and this really does add a new dimension of excitement to pike fishing.

There are two important ingredients for success with this approach:- one which we cannot predict, but the other we can.

Willingness to take the fly

The first ingredient is that the pike must be in the mood to have a go. Or, at least, they must be willing to be persuaded! This is essential, because a pike lying on the bottom will have to cover the entire depth of the lake to take a bait on the surface, and sometimes the fish will simply not be tempted up. It's far better to change to a sinking line and get down among the fish than persevere at the surface without a result.

There are many factors which govern the willingness of a pike to leave its lair to take a bait. The time of year, the weather, when the last meal was eaten, the temperature of the water, the time of day, and many more. It is very difficult to predict the level of willingness on a given day, and no-one would claim to be able to do so. Sometimes, fishing the surface will produce a fish every few casts whereas on other days, with apparently similar conditions, little or nothing is caught. This unpredictability also applies when comparing one lake with another. Once, I spent a whole morning surface fishing a lake without any success. I didn't even see a fish. My route home took me past another lake, which was only a mile away from the first, and I stopped for a few casts. I took two fish in ten minutes, using exactly the same method and the same fly!

Having said all of that, factors such as weather and season do have a significant bearing on the behaviour of pike, and they should always be considered. It is worth remembering, though, that pike are much less fickle than trout, and aren't nearly so affected by adverse weather conditions. For example, if I had to fish on a scorching hot summer's day I would be much more confident of catching a pike than a trout.

Calm weather

The other requirement for successful surface fishing is calm weather. This method comes into its own on those days when the water is like a mirror, or only slightly ruffled by a whisper of wind. Pike depend a lot on their excellent vision, (and fly fishing is entirely visual in its appeal) so half the battle is just getting the pike to spot your fly. There is no better way to achieve this than to fish the surface on a calm day. Any surface disturbance immediately draws attention to the fly, and because it is high up off the bottom it is visible across a much wider area of lake bed than a fly fished deep. This is, I think, the principal reason why this method is so successful on the right day. Clear water is also an advantage as it affords the pike greater visual range.

Tackle

A very slow sink shooting head and a long leader of six to eight feet are the principal tackle requirements. Slow sinkers vary a lot in sink rate, and if the line sinks too fast it will prevent the whole cast being fished out on the surface. Intermediates are suitable, especially for very slow retrieves and long casting, but it can be frustrating having to wait for the line to sink sufficiently before the retrieve can begin. Fishing with a shorter leader will reduce the wait. I use flies of varying buoyancy in order to produce different actions and degrees of surface disturbance. Extra buoyancy will produce a more vigorous action and more disturbance.

The Wakefly method

The most straightforward method is to cast out and begin the retrieve almost immediately. The intermediate sinks a few inches so the line doesn't create a disturbance on the surface, but the buoyant fly leaves a very attractive wake on a calm surface. As every pike angler knows, this can be deadly on the right day, especially over open, shallow water where the bottom is weeded up. In overgrown water, this method enables the angler to fish out 'windows' among water lilies, and lots of water can be covered in a short time with a boat.

This is the 'standard' approach to surface fishing for pike, and it imitates a small fish swimming just under the surface. It is especially productive in the situations described above due to the fact that the pike will often lie near the surface under the lily pads, and will strike the fly as it moves close by. The same applies in shallow water when pike will lie hidden on a weedy bottom.

Almost any speed of retrieve will produce fish in these circumstances - anywhere between very fast and dead slow. I have found stopping dead in mid-retrieve for a few seconds can be very effective, with the take often coming as soon as the fly moves off again. The fly can be fished right on the surface, or just under, so that it puts up a bow wave without actually breaking the surface.

Limping method

This is my favourite method of all. In deeper water, the pike is not afforded the ambush opportunities of shallow water. A food fish swimming along under the surface will flee if approached by a pike, so most pike won't bother leaving the bottom to chase a healthy food fish - or, for that matter, a healthy looking wakefly! A little bit more persuasion is required to get them up off the bottom to investigate.

The secret of success is to make the fly imitate a wounded fish. A fish that struggles along, breaking the surface again and again, screams out 'Injured!' and 'Easy meal!', and it will get all the pike in the vicinity stirred up and standing on their fins, ready to charge! That means no fast bursts of speed. Dead slow and stop, full stop. The retrieve must be constantly varied, and it is essential for the angler to watch the fly throughout the retrieve in order to produce a life-like action in the fly. The slow pace of the retrieve gives the pike lots of time to get interested and make an attack.

Once the cast has been made, wait for the line to sink a foot or two. At this point, a few short pulls will take the fly under the surface and pausing or slowing the retrieve will allow the fly to swim slowly up towards the top, nose first. Just as it breaks surface, a gentle pull will cause it to turn downwards and dive again, leaving a tempting swirl on the surface. A few jerks will cause more disturbance and a short dive, then a pause will allow the fly to head for the surface once more. You can make your fly rest awhile on the surface, twitching, before repeating the process. When the water is flat calm I like to keep the fly just beneath the surface. As the fly rises head first towards the surface, a short pull on the line at the critical moment will cause it to turn downwards just before it breaks surface, leaving a tell-tale boil on the top. This produces a tremendously life-like action which accounts for a lot of fish. With practice, you will perfect your skill at imitating a struggling fish, but it demands concentration. Changing the fly for one with more or less buoyancy will produce a different action, and sometimes this will make all the difference to success. I have also noticed that flies tied with finer bucktail produce a better action for this kind of fishing.

Fishing in this way is a very enjoyable and engrossing pursuit in itself, as it produces a superbly realistic imitation of a wounded fish. But be careful not to get too engrossed - takes can be frightening, especially on a calm day close to the boat! Of all the methods I use, this one seems to induce the most confident takes from the pike. Usually the fish will charge the fly from below, slamming into it with abandon. On other occasions, takes will be very gentle indeed. The great strength of slowly working a fly across a calm surface is that a big pike can watch it for a considerable time before it moves out of view, and often the fish will cruise up to investigate, instead of charging. Stopping dead for four or five seconds is usually the key to bringing a fish up, and resuming the retrieve will normally provoke the strike. Once, when I was fishing in mirror calm conditions, I saw a very slight movement in the water around my static fly. I wasn't sure if I had imagined it or not, so I paused for a few more seconds, and, lo and behold, a pike made a perfect head and tail rise to my fly, engulfing it gently, just like a big trout taking a hatching buzzer. It was one of my most pleasing pike ever! Firstly, she was tempted up off the bottom, then she took time to inspect the fly, and satisfied, she took it confidently and at her leisure. I must say that my confidence in the Ballydoolagh Bomber rose about ten notches after that!

Fishing mid-water
Quick - stop. Quick - quick - stop. This approach most resembles spinning for pike with artificial lure and fixed spool reel or multiplier. To my mind, it is the least interesting, yet on its day it can be very productive. Some may wonder why I don't just spin for the pike and enjoy being able to cast a decent distance. Apart from the aesthetic advantage of fly fishing, there is another advantage that this approach has over spinning.

My experience of fishing for trout has taught me that larger fish take more tempting than their less experienced siblings. As I have already said, many a large trout has been hooked by accident when the rod was set down, leaving the flies to slowly sink through the water, whereas hours of steady retrieving had produced nothing. These, and many other situations lead me to believe that a larger, more experienced fish is less likely to strike impulsively at a briskly retrieved lure than a smaller one. They seem to want more time to inspect the bait and choose to accept or reject it. The fact that I have had far more large trout follow my fly without taking it than small ones further supports this conclusion.

The pike are no different - the larger fish will need more persuading to leave the bottom and chase a lure in mid-water. I believe that the ability to slow down or stop the lure for a few seconds - and still look appealing - is an invaluable aid in tempting big fish. When a food fish pauses, it neither sinks nor floats upwards, but sits static in the water, and the Ballydoolagh Bomber can imitate this accurately, whereas a lure will just sink.

Using a fast sink line and a low buoyancy fly, it is possible to cover a lot of water in a relatively short time, and the quick-quick-stop variation is certainly a productive approach. A sudden pause during a quick retrieve to let the fly sit static in mid-water for four or five seconds will often induce a strike. Imagine a big pike eyeing it up as it hovers. The fast retrieve caught her attention and now she is watching intently as it sits suspended above. Two sharp pulls on the line cause the fins of the pike to stand up in readiness, and as the fly stops again, the pike seizes the opportunity to leap forwards and upwards, slamming into the bait. Bingo! Pike find it irresistible! The downward pull of the sinking line and the buoyancy of the fly will cause the fly to sit virtually still in the water, just like a real fish.

I usually employ this method over deeper water where the bottom is unfishable. It is also my first choice if I want to cover a lot of water, especially if I am in a drifting boat. I use a fast sink shooting head for a relatively brisk retrieve, or a standard sink shooting head for slower speeds and shallower water. Either way, the pause is often the trigger that brings the bigger fish up to take the fly.

I have used Al's Eel more and more in recent times for both surface and mid-water fishing, especially when the going is tough. The extra movement in the body makes a welcome - and often significant - change when things are hard.

Proper application of methods
All the methods described in this book will catch fish through-out the year, but there is no doubt that some are more suited to

particular times of the year than others. Certainly, there may be days in January when every pike in the area wants to eat your surface fly, but these are exceptions. In winter, when the water is cold, the pike will lie on the bottom in a state of lethargy most of the time. Fast sink line, four foot leader and a dead slow retrieve will usually be your best option.

Likewise, the surface or mid-water fly will work far better when the pike are hungry, and willing to have a go. This is usually spring and autumn, as well as the cooler summer days. Far more water can be covered with these methods, and so they will produce more fish on certain days than deep and slow.

Within these general guidelines, however, there is infinite variation, and this is what keeps the angler coming back for more. All the methods in this book will have their day, and keeping them in mind will greatly enhance your chances of success, especially when the action is slow. The greatest angling pleasure is often gained by catching a fish after making a thoughtful change in approach because the 'standard' method has failed to produce.

Al's eel produces a vigorous action in the water.

CHAPTER 10

BIG PIKE

There is no doubt that big pike spend most of their time lying in deep water. Of course, larger specimens can be caught in shallow water, especially at certain times of the year, but if you want to maximise your chances of taking large pike on the fly throughout the year, you will spend much of your time fishing in deeper water.

When I say deep water I mean more than six feet. Pike may lie in forty or fifty feet of water, or even deeper, but most of the larger specimens can be taken in water which is between six and twenty feet deep. In my experience, the most productive depth range for bigger fish is between six and fifteen feet.

You will also spend most of your time fishing a slow retrieve, especially in winter or high summer, when the fish are lethargic and require more persuasion. Big pike will usually require more coaxing to strike at a lure than their junior brothers. The only predictable exception to these rules is at spawning time, when most of the pike's instinct for self-preservation seems to be shelved.

Fishing during the spawning season
The most productive times of the year for pike are undoubtedly the weeks before and after spawning, when the requirement for food is at its highest, and the fish are in shallow water. It seems that some pike will even feed right up to and around the actual event of spawning. Last March, my friend John Todd chaperoned a distinguished party of pike anglers on a sortie to Lough Erne - Neville Fickling, Mick Brown and Chris Tarrant among them. Their biggest fish weighed a fraction under 30lbs, and was taken in three feet of chocolate brown water on

ledgered herring. The fish had only just finished spawning - the last few eggs were still falling out as she was landed.

Depending on climate, pike will begin to move in and out of the shallows in late February or early March, driven by the urge to spawn. A rise in the water level will often bring on spawning, which, by the way, is said to coincide with the spawning activities of frogs. (The pike will even eat frog spawn during this time.) They choose weedy bays with muddy bottoms, and spawn in a few inches of water, often at the back of weed beds when the water is high.

The pike will feed voraciously both before and after spawning, but I have never been keen on catching pike before they have spawned. The last thing a fifteen year old, spawn-laden, hen fish needs is to fight for her life just before she begins the hard work of laying two hundred thousand plus eggs. It's something akin to asking a heavily pregnant woman to run the race of her life in an Olympic final! I suppose my background in game angling has taught me that fish should be left alone during the most stressful and exhausting of all their activities.

Having said that, it is clear that the spawning activities of the pike are not nearly so traumatic as they are for salmon or trout. By the time a trout has fought its way up river, spent a few months living in an environment it's not used to, made do with less food, endured the stresses of digging up gravel with its tail, spawned, and then made its way back down into the lake it came from, it is thoroughly spent. All the pike has to do is simply cruise into its spawning ground and deposit its eggs or milt. Early on in my pike fishing career I was often amazed at how hard a big hen pike could fight only a week or two after she had spawned, and this helped allay any qualms I had about fishing for spring pike.

Locating big pike
It might sound obvious, but the first task in catching big pike

is to find the big pike. We have just established that this is easiest at spawning time, as the pike will choose the same bays year after year to spawn in, but it is not so straightforward at other times when the pike are scattered. There is no use in fishing a bay that never produces a double when around the point there is a hotspot which regularly yields twenty pounders. Getting to know the water is very important.

Even so, good knowledge of the water does not automatically guarantee success. Pike do not conform rigidly to established behaviour patterns, and on different waters habits can vary considerably. Additionally, and as all anglers know only too well, behaviour can vary from day to day, even though the weather and other conditions seem to remain constant. Success with big fish requires experience - experience both of pike fishing in general, and of spending time on the same water so that a knowledge of the lies and feeding patterns can be learned and kept up to date.

Despite all these variables, many of the pike's general behaviour patterns have been well documented and it will be helpful to look at some of these here. Approaching any water with these rules in mind will greatly improve your chances of success.

Rule 1: Find the walls

Pike love to have their 'backs to the wall'. Any feature, such as an underwater drop-off, the edge of a weed bed or a sunken tree will be a likely spot for big pike. Pike are hunted as well as being the hunter, and even big pike, which have no natural enemies, like the security afforded by good cover. The largest fish of all may well be found where there is cover on more than one side, such as a hole in the bank or a man made object which they can hide in. It is worth remembering that the bigger fish will always take the best lies.

Many years ago, at the Queen Mother Reservoir in west

London, some thieves stripped out a stolen car and pushed the shell into the water, minus doors and windows. It soon became a recognised big fish hot spot, because the very largest trout in the vicinity moved into the driving seat, (metaphorically and literally!), to wait for dinner to swim by. Every water has its unique features, and time spent familiarising oneself with these will surely pay dividends in both enjoyment and results.

One of the quickest and most interesting ways to gain this kind of essential information is to get afloat with a fish finder. There are many fully portable fish finders on the market today which are specifically designed for freshwater use, and potential hot spots (as well as the current location of food fish) can be discovered very quickly. There is no better way to 'learn' a new water than with a good fish finder.

The most obvious way to find a big fish hot spot is to look for deep water close to the shore. Often, the lie of the land will give some leading clues, especially where a steep bank or hill runs down to the water. A steep drop-off from the shore provides a natural wall, as well as a convenient choice of depth, and big fish can be expected at such locations.

Rule 2: 'Birds of a feather flock together'

Another interesting habit to remember is that large hen fish like to keep one another's company. Catch one good fish in your swim and its fairly likely that there will be several more nearby. The opposite also holds true -: catch a tiddler and your next fish from the same spot is most likely to be similar in size. At this point the bloke who caught a 'two' and a 'twenty' on successive casts will shout "Rubbish!" Of course, there will always be the exception - and in pike fishing there will be a lot of them! - but we are not claiming hard and fast rules here. These are just general habits which, on certain days, will help us to locate our quarry. If you are after big fish and you have taken two tiddlers on the trot, the best advice is to move. Fish out in the deeper water, or take a walk along the bank. You may only have to travel a short distance before you hit better fish. Of course you may elect to enjoy the sport provided by the smaller fish while you have it! Once again, this total freedom of movement is, for me, one of the most pleasing aspects of fly fishing for pike.

Sometimes, the pike will apply this rule very specifically indeed. Occasionally I have witnessed the situation where just about every pike in the lake is shoaled up in one small area. I recently enjoyed a two week spell on a lake during which the pike were all crammed into one bed of lilies. If I moved only fifty yards away in any direction I would struggle to catch. As an experiment, I spent almost a whole day fishing the entire remainder of the lake, (which was around eighty acres is size) and caught only a few small jacks; the fishing bonanza only resumed when I moved back into the bed of lily pads. Another point of interest was that the larger fish consistently lay in one particular area of the lily pads throughout the period, and every trip produced at least one double from that spot.

Such a phenomenon can take some explaining, but there may be some clues to provide at least a partial answer. This particular situation occurred in May, and the lily patch was close to the bay in which the pike spawn each year. It may be that the pike naturally gravitated towards the cover which water lilies provide in relatively shallow, clear water. Alternatively, the explanation may lie in food supply. Food fish may have congregated in this area (for whatever reason) and such an environment would provide excellent ambush opportunities. (In truth, however, neither of these explanations are adequate, as lily pads only a few yards away were virtually devoid of fish.)

Whatever the reason, the point is that the larger fish consistently kept together in the same area, and this seems to be a fairly common rule among pike.

Rule 3: The kitchen is the heart of the home
Pike and people are no different in this respect - both love their food and tend to gather wherever it is! Locate the pike's larder and you can be pretty sure that pike will not be far away. Finding out this kind of information comes only with experience, and it is certainly easier said than done. Staring out across a large expanse of water often produces very little feedback, but keeping eyes and ears open while you are fishing can make all the difference. Look for fish consistently moving on the surface in one area, or talk to other anglers: match anglers can be a super source of information here. Sometimes a feeding cormorant will betray the presence of a shoal of food fish.

You may also be lucky enough to happen upon a shoal of food fish which is under siege from a posse of hungry pike. Repeated charges send fish jumping in all directions, and the disturbance can be spotted from some considerable distance. This often happens in autumn when the pike are stocking up for the winter, and it is spectacular to watch. If you see such activity, move there immediately! There will be lots of pike to catch and they won't be shy about taking your offering, either! I remember wading a 'big fish' water when I spotted just such an orgy about a hundred yards out, along the shore of a small island. I could only watch in frustration as twenty pounders repeatedly slammed into a shoal of fingerlings. I'd have paid a lot of money to rent a boat at that moment!

Often, the annual migrations of food fish in larger lakes is well documented, and this kind of information is invaluable. Lough Erne, (my local lake), has held several world records for catches of roach, but if you are in the wrong place at the wrong time, you won't even get a bite. In May and June they run a local river to spawn, and at the peak of these runs the riverbed literally turns black with a wall to wall carpeting of roach. Many large catches of pike have been made at the mouth of this river as the pike have learned that a steady supply of fish is available here for weeks on end. They simply take up residence and let the roach come to them.

Information like this on any water is mainly gleaned by talking to other anglers, so a friendly smile or the offer of a cigarette can be good for your fishing, as well as general camaraderie.

Rule 4: Don't put all your eggs in one basket

As we have seen, pike do not always stick to expected behaviour patterns, and therefore it is prudent to expect the unexpected. I once climbed a tree and watched a pike sunbathe in the middle of a deep pond. I had often watched pike sunbathe in shallows, but not over deep water. She was sitting right in the middle of a shoal of four ounce roach, but somehow they knew that she posed no threat at that moment, even though they were within twelve inches of her huge jaws. Not the most common behaviour, you'll agree, but it serves to show that nothing can be assumed when fishing for pike.

If you are fishing hard on the bottom in fifteen feet of water on a cold winter's day, it is reasonable to expect the larger pike to be lying on the bottom. However, this is not always the case. Pike do spend time in mid-water, or patrolling near the surface, and you can sometimes find yourself fishing the wrong water, even though it should be the right water! It is always advisable to vary the chosen pattern of fishing from time to time as this can sometimes produce a surprising result. For example, every fifth cast strip your fly home as soon as it hits the water, or let it sink only half way down and then inch it in. It may seem a waste of time to strip a fly along the surface in fifteen feet of water in the dead of winter, but it only takes a few seconds, and it also provides a little variety to keep interest up. Stranger things have happened than catching a pike in such circumstances. The angler who is willing to vary his tactics, and to give the unlikely (or even the ridiculous!) a try, will do better and learn more than Mr. Middle-of-the-road. The following story is a good example of this.

Several years ago a young lad, with the help of his dad, took his first ever pike - on a treble hook wrapped in a rasher of raw bacon. It was plopped in beside the jetty along a weed bed. It's true - and it weighed twenty one pounds! The fish was caught on a fifty acre lake, which is one of seven lakes which are all on one island. This island is in an even bigger lake, with several hundred other islands on it!

Sounds like a fishy story, doesn't it? But it is true. The lake in question is called Lough Barry, which is on Inishmore island on Lough Erne, which is the third largest lake in the British Isles. Some of the most unlikely angling stories are true, and just about anything can happen in fishing, so varying the approach is the name of the game. Although we may enjoy relating highly unusual variations like the one above, most successful diversions will be of a more sane kind. For example, sometimes an angler will concentrate on fishing the water at the extreme limit of his casting range when all the time a big pike is lying along the rushes by his feet. One of the most common errors I have observed in this respect is with regard to fishing jetties. In Ireland many of our lakes have wooden fishing jetties built for anglers to clear shallow water or weedy margins. Most anglers will just march out to the end of them and begin fishing the water beyond, without realising that the jetty provides ideal cover for a pike, and that they have just disturbed the best lie on the whole shore. I fished a lake recently with two jetties and of the three pike I caught that afternoon, two came from under the jetties. Before using them to stand on, I simply waded out and cast across the front of each jetty.

The Ballydoolagh Bomber rig is extremely versatile and will just as effectively fish a three foot deep weedy margin as a twenty foot deep gully. Every angler should take advantage of this flexibility and vary the approach from time to time during a day's fishing. By taking this thinking approach, we will learn more and improve our catches considerably.

There is no doubt that the angler who considers his approach carefully and learns to read the water well will consistently take big pike, while the unthinking angler must depend on good fortune, and will not be nearly so successful. Although the approach described in this book will improve both the presentation of the fly and the versatility of fly tackle in difficult situations, it will not guarantee success with big pike. Successful angling depends on skill, and, even more, on knowledge of the water being fished, and both can only be learned by spending time out there doing it.

CHAPTER 11

BOAT FISHING

In general, fishing from a boat will give an angler a considerable edge over his counterpart on the bank. All the methods described in this book will be more effective from a boat, due mainly to the fact that more water can be covered. The only proviso to this is that the 'standard' method of fishing the line hard on the bottom requires the boat to be anchored. Attempting this method from a drifting boat is difficult because the speed of retrieve cannot be controlled due to the movement of the boat.

Apart from the obvious advantages of using a boat, there are several effective methods worth remembering which cannot be used by the bank angler.

Fishing the walls
We have already established that good pike are likely to be found wherever sudden changes in depth occur. The first thing an experienced pike angler fishing a new water will look for will be shelves, ledges, edges of weed beds and any other feature providing a steep depth contour. A boat will allow an angler to find hotspots that a bank angler would never discover. Take full advantage of this mobility to discover and fish these areas.

The most obvious place, of course, is near to the bank, as there is always some sort of drop off here! Usually there is more that one place where the bank gives way to relatively deep water in a short distance, and these are common hotspots for pike. (I learned this lesson many years ago when I deadbaited a new water without success - until I explored the water close in to the bank. I found it was nearly twenty feet deep under my rod tip. My next cast was not a cast at all - I simply opened the bail arm and let the bait sink to the bottom. I was rewarded with an eight pounder which took the dead roach on the way down.)

Anchoring fifteen or twenty yards off shore and casting the fly into deep water close to the shore can be a productive method for big pike. Keep an extremely vigilant watch on the line as the fly is dragged into the depths - sometimes a pike will grab it as it swims downwards. As the contours of the underwater bank become familiar, a little tug here and there will allow the fly to fish close to the bank all the way down.

Of course, with a boat one can explore the whole bed of the lake, and gain access to ledges and drop-offs which are out of reach to the shore angler. Such places are often patrolled by very large pike and are well worth a little perseverance in discovering. Keeping a light rope handy with a weight on one end is an effective depth gauge. I put one turn of insulating tape five feet from the weight, two at ten feet and so on. This makes it easy to read the depth at a glance, and hooking the rope round a rowlock at a fixed depth will avoid the necessity of letting it all the way down and then hauling it all the way up every time you test the depth. A fish finder will do the job even better. Whichever you use, use it regularly, because it will provide vital information.

I have not yet made up my mind as to whether fish finders are a good thing or not. They certainly do reduce the skill and intuition needed to read a water, and such ability can only be learned and developed over a number of years. On the other hand, they do cut the learning curve on a new water by half . . . I don't really know. I don't come out in one camp or the other. Either way, fish finders are here to stay, and each angler must make up his own mind.

Trolling the fly
The traditional method of trolling a lure is still one of the most popular methods of taking pike in Ireland. Many anglers are

quite happy to sit in a boat all day, listening to the outboard engine and waiting for the rod to jump in its mount as a salmon, trout or pike grabs the spoon bait that is swimming forty yards behind the boat. Not the most exciting fishing in the world, but it does produce some good sport, and many large pike are caught by this method on the loughs of Ireland.

Trolling the fly is also a very effective way of taking pike. The only important difference is that the speed of the boat must be considerably slower than for trolling with spoons and spinners. The relatively thick fly line is easily lifted in the water by lateral movement and this lift is greatly increased at speed. There is no doubt, however, that the slower trolling speed needed for the fly is a distinct advantage in most situations.

Another advantage is that the buoyancy of the fly will cause it to swim slightly higher in the water than the lowest part of the belly in the line. This effect can be accentuated by increasing the length of the leader, and this lends a considerable advantage when fishing close to the bottom by helping to avoid snags that a spoon bait would not.

I rarely troll for pike, but when I do I always use a lead core line and troll from a drifting boat on a windy day. Using an out-board motor is not feasible. Sometimes I have tied on a second leader of about a foot long and attached an Arsley bomb to keep the fly close to the bottom in deep water. I always 'work' the fly to impart a life-like action.

Choosing a boat for pike fishing
In Ireland we are blessed with a seemingly endless number and variety of lakes. Many are small and remote, with weedy margins and soft bottoms. These provide ideal habitat for pike and present the angler with a truly wonderful opportunity. It is very easy to pick a small lough from an ordnance survey map and be the first angler to wet a line on it in months. Many of these lakes produce huge fish - I know of two local lakes, both

under fifty acres in size, which have yielded 40lb fish in the past few years to livebait.

Of course, one has to gain access to these forgotten lakes, and many are quite simply unfishable from the shore. A boat is the only answer, but getting the right boat for the job is essential. There is a bewildering variety of small boats on the market, and I have made a few mistakes that may help prevent a first time buyer from making a poor choice.

Canoe or dinghy?

Canadian canoes are becoming very popular in this country, and their rugged 'outback' image has persuaded many people to buy them for this sort of work. Nevertheless, my advice is to avoid them, unless you are well used to being on the water and are a good swimmer! They are, for most European tastes, just too jittery and cramped for comfortable fly casting. They are also prone to blow around all over the lake at the slightest puff of wind, and are both heavy and awkward to carry. I bought one to see how it would shape up, but the results were disappointing.

Which dinghy?

A dinghy of between seven and ten feet is a much better choice, but choosing a dinghy is not as straightforward as it might seem. For this kind of work, the most important factor is weight. A heavy boat is a pain to load and unload, especially if it's on a roof rack, and things get even worse when it must be carried several hundred yards to the lake.

The four most common materials for dinghies are fibreglass, wood, aluminium and plastic, and plastic is by far the best material to choose. Fibreglass is heavy and brittle, aluminium is expensive and cold, while wood is fragile and requires a lot of maintenance. Plastic is very tough, as well as being lightweight and cheap, and is by far the best choice. Most plastic boats also have built in buoyancy, which is absolutely essential.

There are two basic shapes: the cathedral type dinghy (with a square front), and the more conventional clinker shape with a pointed prow. The cathedral type will accommodate two anglers more comfortably, whereas the conventional hull is more seaworthy if it blows up rough. Some dinghies have a catamaran type hull instead of the standard flat bottom or clinker shapes, and this significantly improves stability, especially when leaning to one side.

Some modern plastic boats can be bought with a permanent roller wheel built into the transom. Instead of dragging the boat along the ground, simply lift it at the front and the rear end trundles along behind on the roller. This feature is a great bonus, as the boat will more often than not have to be transported across a field or two to the lake. Simply load all the gear into the boat and 'wheelbarrow' the whole lot to the water's edge.

Add-on rollers can also be purchased for fitting to standard dinghies and are available from boat chandlers.

Of all the boats I have looked at and tried out, the BiC 252 has the best combination of features, and I am exceedingly happy with mine.

Accessories

In addition to boat and oars, you will need a lifejacket or buoyancy aid. This is a vital piece of equipment for a small boat, especially in winter.

An anchor is also essential. Half a concrete block or a large stone tied on the end of a length of rope will, in my opinion, make a better anchor for this type of fishing than any you will buy. The reason for this is that you will often be anchored over mud, and an ordinary anchor will simply drag along the bottom as it has nothing to grip. There are few things more frustrating than an anchor that won't hold! A stone will sink down into the mud and hold firm against a stiff breeze.

Finally, a word on safety. Take great care when going out on windy days, as small boats are extremely difficult to handle in a strong breeze and never, ever take a small dinghy out on a big water in windy conditions.

CHAPTER 12

RIVER FISHING

There is lots of excellent pike fishing to be enjoyed on rivers, and they present a new and interesting challenge for the fly fisher. Rivers vary enormously in character and size, as do the species that inhabit them, so investigating all the options and variations would take a book in itself, and this is not our purpose here. We shall only take a quick look at river fishing, not least because most pike anglers would choose a lake in preference to a river as a hunting ground for big pike.

Before all the river anglers begin jumping up and down, let me qualify what I mean when I say 'river fishing'. I'm not talking about really big rivers that sweep into huge bends and have large areas of slack water with boats motoring up and down. To all intents and purposes, these can be approached and fished like a lake, and much of the information in this book will apply to such rivers. It is the smaller rivers that are the subject here: those which have little or no boat traffic or where the water is interspersed with shallow runs and deep pools.

One cannot expect to consistently take large pike from such rivers, but the sense of the hunt and the requirement to stalk out the prey, together with the need to 'read' the river, more than makes up for the smaller size of the quarry. These fish are generally leaner and fitter than their lake counterparts, too. This kind of fly fishing for pike is the closest to trout fishing in its approach and execution.

Many anglers who choose to go fly fishing for pike will already be competent anglers in their own field, and will need little advice regarding where to find pike in the river, so we shall keep advice to basics. The main rule is to fish in deep, slack water, especially near to sharp drop offs such as a weir, or a steep bank on the outside of a bend. However, do not neglect the shallows too much, particularly in spring or early summer, when pike can sometimes be observed sunning themselves.

My tackle for the river is most often the medium or fast sink shooting head, Ballydoolagh Bomber, and a short leader of about three feet. This gives me the ability to draw the fly under within a few seconds of it landing on the water, which is essential in a restricted area. Many of the deeper holding pools are relatively small, and a fly landing on the water is often spotted immediately. In these circumstances I find that the ability to hold the fly static just under the surface is very effective. Imagine a pike focusing its attention on a non-descript object that has just landed on the surface. After a few seconds it suddenly comes to life and breaks through into the environment below, swimming down a few inches and then rests just under the surface like a real fish. The pike are usually impressed, and the sight of the fish hitting the fly is thrilling. It is the short leader that permits the fly to be activated early, as well as making the whole rig more manageable in moving water.

Where the water is shallower, say under three or four feet, I do not usually allow the whole rig to settle on the bottom. The current may prevent the fly being fished properly, and often branches and other debris washed down in floods will be the first thing you catch! Of course, in large holding pools where the water is virtually static it is possible to allow the whole lot to settle on the bottom and inch it home, but often it is helpful to keep things higher up in the water.

It really does not matter whether you fish upstream or down. The current will almost always be very slow in pikey looking spots, and the retrieve must be relied upon to impart life to the fly, not the current.

For the most part, a common sense application of the methods in this book will see the aspiring river angler through most difficulties, and experience of your own particular river will be your greatest asset in tempting its pike!

CHAPTER 13

Standard Methods of Fly Fishing for Pike

Fly fishing for pike is not new. For centuries anglers have used large flies to catch pike, and a fair bit has already been written on the subject. Despite this, the art of fly fishing for pike has remained fairly primitive, especially when compared to the many sophisticated techniques for catching trout which have been developed. Until recently, things have not progressed much beyond casting out a large lure and stripping it home, interspersed with the odd pause or tweak.

Interest in catching pike on the fly has really taken off in the past decade, and the tactics described in this book are, I hope, a step forward in the development of the sport. I have certainly experienced a revival in both my enjoyment and success since I began developing the buoyant fly\sinking line combination for pike fishing. Not only that, I have found this approach to be at least as productive as spinning. I have often fished against another angler using plugs and spoons from the same boat, in order to compare the effectiveness of both methods. Usually, the fly proves to be more successful, especially on difficult days. I have caught pike on worms, spinners, plugs, live bait, dead bait, trout flies, and purpose-tied lures, but fishing with a buoyant fly on a variety of sinking lines provides unmatched flexibility, enjoyment and effectiveness.

Having said that, I do believe the conventional sunk fly is an essential weapon in the fly fisher's armoury. The Ballydoolagh Bomber will not sink, and from time to time this is a distinct disadvantage. Fishing in extremely tight situations, such as in very small windows among lily pads may be difficult with a buoyant fly if the pike are lying on the bottom. A floating line and a sinking fly will often work better, especially if there is not enough room to allow the whole Ballydoolagh Bomber rig to sink.

Regular pike flies can also be fished in a sink and draw fashion with a floating line, and this, I think, is their greatest appeal. If I had to go pike fishing with just one other type of fly I would choose a Bunny Leech, which is essentially a 10-15cm rabbit fur strip tied to a weighted hook. This combination produces a remarkably fluent movement in the water when fished using a series of short pulls, with a pause between each to allow the hook to sink. This sink and draw action imparts a vigorous, roller-coaster movement in the body as it follows the rise and fall of the weighted head. It is especially useful in coloured water, where lots of movement maximises the chances of the fly being spotted.

Of course, Al's Eel is tied with rabbit fur strip and it will produce an undulating action in the water, but the effect is greatly exaggerated with a weighted hook. This is due to the fact that a weighted head will sink much faster than a foam head will rise. Thus, a much more energetic action can be imparted to the fly without speeding up the retrieve. This greatly increases the likelihood of catching the attention of any nearby pike, while the slow overall speed of retrieve provides lots of time for the fish to make a strike.

I once spent a day pike fishing with Ed Jaworowski, a well-known American salt water fly fisherman, and I witnessed the effectiveness of this method for the first time. He easily outperformed me and my Ballydoolagh Bomber using heavily weighted Bunny Leeches. We were fishing in shallow, cloudy water and the animated movement of his fly attracted far more pike than my Ballydoolagh Bomber. (Come to think of it, his success may also have had something to do with the fact that he is one of the top fly fishers in America!) I have used this tactic to great effect since, and it definitely works better than buoyant flies in certain conditions. On the down side, these flies are very heavy and difficult to cast any distance; I usually only use them when I'm in a boat.

The problems with conventional pike flies

There have been lots of new attempts at pike flies over the years, including my own, but most of them have had serious drawbacks. Many are too small to interest big fish, and the larger patterns can be difficult to cast. This is usually down to either too much weight or excessive bulk, or both. Casting some popular patterns more than fifteen yards is an achievement, and even then, each cast is a struggle. Heavy flies are also very dangerous, and I wouldn't cast some of these 'blocks' without wearing glasses.

(The Ballydoolagh Bomber does not retain any water, thanks to the absence of fur, dubbing or marabou in the tying, and this makes it very user-friendly. The fly is both streamlined and light, even when it has just been lifted out of the water. It can easily be cast twenty five or thirty yards with a shooting head, and even further with a brisk following wind. The only conventional pike flies that have similar casting qualities to the Ballydoolagh Bomber are very small ones!)

I have also found that many pike flies have no stomach for the pike's teeth, and are destroyed after only a few pike. (This continues to be a problem though, because even the toughest flies will eventually succumb.) Complexity can also be a drawback - some of the Continental tyings I have come across require a degree in fly tying, as well as an hour or two for each fly!

Very few patterns are both practical to tie and durable. To my mind, the most common mistake is to include too many elements in the fly, which increases weight, bulk and complexity without providing any significant advantage in appeal. I always keep these factors in mind when experimenting with new patterns.

Tying regular pike flies

Pike flies can be tied from just about any material which comes to hand. Whole feathers, goat hair, squirrel, polar bear, calf tail, marabou, rabbit, synthetic materials - you name it and it's worth experimenting with. People have caught pike on frog, newt, rat, and a variety of other imitations, and one can spend endless hours developing and experimenting with these. And why not, if it takes your fancy? However, it is worth remembering that the pike's diet is mainly made up of fish, and I think it is a good general rule to aim in that direction, at least initially. When tying fish imitations, the golden rule is to remember that all fish are dark on top, gradually getting lighter towards the bottom. Remember this and you will not go far wrong with your experiments.

Favourite hooks

Effective flies can be tied on treble hooks, tubes, or large singles. I have experimented with all of these, and I now exclusively use large single hooks. Apart from the fact that too much damage is inflicted by trebles, there are several other good reasons for using singles. As I have just pointed out, fish are always dark on top and light on the bottom. With a large single, the hook bend acts like a keel, ensuring that the correct attitude is maintained in the water, and your carefully tied roach imitation will not be swimming around upside down! A treble will sit any old way, so presentation cannot be controlled in the same way. Of course, if you're trying to emulate an injured fish it might actually be desirable for your fly to swim upside down!

I also think that a treble can strangle the fight out of a pike. Many times a treble will bed itself into the upper and lower jaws, holding the mouth firmly closed. If a fish cannot breathe, (and a fish must open its mouth to breathe), it will tire much quicker due to a lack of oxygen. I use size 4\0 almost exclusively.

Favourite body materials

A fly that is tied from whole feathers provides one of the best all-round combinations of durability, flexibility and lightness. Long cock saddle feathers of 10-15 cms are best, and can be used effectively on all types of fly.

Bucktail is the best material for imitating fish bodies, both in shape and movement. It's not the toughest of materials, but taking a little extra care when extracting a bucktail fly from a pike's mouth will greatly lengthen its life.

Rabbit fur strips are unrivalled for providing fluent, life-like movement in the water, especially when fished sink and draw. This is my favourite 'enticer' material, and it also stands up exceptionally well to the pike's teeth.

Marabou provides exceptional movement in the water, but it is delicate, and soaks up water like a sponge. It is best used in combination with other materials.

Favourite patterns

The Bunny Leech

Hook: Heavy (or weighted) single, size 4\0.
Body: Rabbit fur strip, about 15cms long, 3-4mm wide. Any colour.
Head: Marabou, short bucktail or large hackle. Any colour.

Ed Jawarowski's variant of *Lefty's Deceiver* is also an excellent pike fly.

Hook: Large single, size 4\0.
Body: Eight long white cock saddle feathers, laid back to back and tied in (on a vertical axis) to form the body.
Head: Black bucktail, spun on the shank.

One of my best 'regular' patterns is tied with ten feathers, and it is both durable and easy to cast. I call it the *Blackbird* and the tying is as follows:

Hook: Large single, size 4\0.

Body: Up to ten long black cock saddle feathers, tied in randomly by the butts to form a body.

Hackle: Large black cock hackle, wound almost to the eye.

Head: Bunch of squirrel, tied in by the tips in the fashion of a hair wing. Leave 5mm of yellow tips protruding beyond the eye of the hook, and then tie these back on themselves to form a bright spot which resembles an eye. Alternatively, trim off, whip finish a head and paint on eyes.

CHAPTER 14

A Practical Approach

When I go fishing, I want to fish. I absolutely hate spending my time messing about with endless bits of kit, tackle, and aids that add as much hassle as they save. 'Keep it simple, keep it sweet' is the best option for me. I love turning up at the lake and within two minutes I'm all set up and fishing, while the tackle addict has just finished unpacking the car and is searching through all those pockets and bags for the keys. I avoid complexity because it means less bits to carry around and worry about - simplicity is wonderfully user-friendly and saves lots of time!

Flies

I carry one or two simple wallets with a good cross-section of flies in them. I couldn't find anything on the market which was suitable for storing large flies, so I made my own wallet. It permits the flies to be stored in an orderly fashion and carefully viewed before selection, and it is extremely simple to make. In the next chapter I will tell you how.

Binbag

I take a black bin liner if I intend to bring fish home for the table.

Leaders

I put a few spare mono leaders neatly wrapped into coils in my fly pouch, under the foam tray. As a backup, I also carry a spool of hard nylon and a small spool of ten or twelve lb. leader so I can tie up traces to suit the situation when required.

Pliers

Never, ever, go pike fishing without bringing pointed-nosed pliers or artery forceps. It is impossible to regularly unhook pike by hand without damaging either the hand or the fish. My personal preference is for the pliers.

Spare spools

I always take a spare spool with a slow sinking shooting head. When the pike can be taken on the surface the opportunity is not to be missed! As I have already said, it is the most exhilarating method of catching pike - full stop! - and I can quickly change over to fish the surface when conditions suit. I also carry a lead core shooting head for really deep water. All the spools are interchangeable with my fly reel, so swapping over takes only a minute or two.

Buoyancy aid

I have one of those trout fishing waist jackets that doubles up as a buoyancy aid, and I always wear it when I'm pike fishing. I have my hook hone and nail clippers permanently attached, and they are very useful. Snagging the fly on a rock can easily turn the hook point over, rendering it virtually useless, and we have already noted the importance of keeping a good point on the hook. I also find my nail clippers handy when I have thick monofilament to cut - they save my teeth! (I prefer nail clippers to scissors as they are much quicker and give a closer cut.)

Apart from these benefits, the main reason for wearing the jacket is for safety. In twenty five years of fishing I have never fallen in, but I do know several people who have, and it is extremely dangerous. An angler drowned recently on one of the trout lakes which I often fish. He was a fit, responsible angler, and an excellent swimmer, but when he fell off the jetty into ten feet of water, there was no-one at hand to help him. He was wearing thigh waders, and these are thought to have caused the drowning. Familiarity does breed contempt, and we only have to stop and think about the consequences of falling in to realise how dangerous it actually is, especially in winter.

Waders
There are four different types of wader on the market today: rubber, PVC sandwich, neoprene and breathable fabrics such as Goretex. All have their relative merits and weaknesses. Neoprene waders are unbearably hot in summer if you have any distance at all to walk. They are also the most difficult to put on. On the other hand, they are by far the warmest when wading in cold water.

Rubber waders are more affordable, but their main weakness is that they are prone to perishing. Once the rubber perishes, they are only fit for the bin. Cheaper versions will last you no more than a season, if you are lucky, and are best avoided. Good quality rubber waders are expensive, and they will certainly last longer, but in my opinion they are not good value for money.

A much better buy is the more recent PVC garment, made from a PVC\nylon\PVC sandwich. These don't rot or perish, and they are much lighter than rubber. They are also cheap to buy and easy to repair.

The fourth type is a relatively recent arrival, made from breathable fabric. This type of material is extremely light and comfortable, being mainly suited to the summer fisherman who does a lot of walking and needs to keep cool. I have never owned a pair of Goretex waders, but I have gone through several Goretex coats and I cannot help wondering if the material might be a little delicate for waders. They are also the most expensive by some margin. Having said that, I have heard many anglers rave about them, and I understand big improvements have been made recently in their ability to resist puncture.

Waders fall into three main designs: thigh waders, chest waders, and the more recent trouser waders. Thigh waders are the most limiting for several reasons. They do not permit deep wading, and often the angler is tempted to ride his luck with the high waterline. If you manage to avoid letting water in over the top, you'll probably get wet anyway when it rains, especially if you are sitting in a boat. Most fishing coats are not long enough to clear the tops of thigh waders, and the water tends to run off the coat directly onto your jeans. Wet bums and thigh waders are just about synonymous!

Chest waders will allow the deepest wading, but they can be uncomfortable to wear all day. It is also impractical to wear a waist coat over them, not only because it increases discomfort, but also because it will get soaked if you use your chest waders to chest wade! In the event, few anglers feel comfortable when wading right up to their chests, and it becomes difficult to cast comfortably or accurately.

Trouser waders are a compromise between the first two types. They have no shoulder straps, are far more comfortable than chest waders, and will accommodate a waistcoat. I have owned all three kinds and I think the trouser wader is the best all round compromise. My choice is for the PVC sandwich type, which only loses out significantly to neoprene on warmth. To compensate, it is possible to wear several pairs of tracksuit bottoms and heavy socks in winter. These layers also absorb body moisture, making things much less clammy than neoprene. The best combination of value, design and quality is the Snowbee version with the Velcro waist belt.

Polarised glasses
Most experienced fly fishers will be aware of the value of polarised glasses. These cut out reflected light from the water's surface, and are a must, especially if you are fishing the surface.

Spring balance
This is an important piece of kit if you like to record your catch,

though I have never carried one on pike fishing trips until recently. There are several reasons for this. First, I only ever kill small pike for the table, and these are not worth weighing. It is now illegal to kill pike over 4kg weight in Northern Ireland, and such fish are too big for eating anyway. If I want to weigh a big pike properly, a sling must also be carried along with the spring balance - more gear. If I go to the bother of weighing it I'll also want a camera to record the catch. And of course, as I am often alone, I'll need a tripod of some kind to set up the shot. Easiest option - don't bother with any of it. Just go and enjoy the fishing!

I suppose, if I am absolutely frank, I would admit to regretting this approach, especially since I started writing this book! I have very few records or photos of fish caught and I don't even know how heavy my biggest ever pike was! I must confess, though, that since I started writing this book I have begun to carry a spring balance in the hope of recording a big catch before publication!

After many, many fishing trips I have whittled away all that I consider to be non-essential, but I'm sure you will choose to add or omit items from my list according to your own requirements. I still change this list from time to time, but as I am a fan of the highly mobile approach, I can't see myself adding a lot more to it.

That's how it is for me. The whole point of angling is the angler's enjoyment, so the best policy is to take what you want and not what others think you should!

CHAPTER 15

Helpful Hints

Casting with a shooting head
Any caster can become competent with a shooting head in a short time.

Start off by casting as normal, as though using a convention-al line. Once the ten yards of fly line is out through the end ring, the final cast, or shoot, can be performed. Essentially, this is a standard forward cast, which is aimed a little higher than usual. The line will shoot out until it lands on the water, pulling the backing out through the rings after it. Avoid work-ing extra line out in an attempt to gain more distance on the shoot - this usually results in a shorter cast. The best casts are made with only one or two yards of backing out through the last rod ring when the shoot is made.

As you get the hang of this, you can learn how to 'single haul', a technique which will significantly improve your distance. Single hauling is simply pulling down sharply on the backing at a critical moment during the shoot in order to increase the line speed through the air. The critical moment is when the rod is loaded to its maximum on the forward cast. Only a short quick pull of about a foot is required, and timing, not strength, will bring success.

Once this skill has been learned it will prove invaluable, not only for pike fishing but for trout fishing too, especially on those days of high summer or deep winter when trout hug the bottom. And if you ever take up salt water fly fishing, it will get you off to an excellent start.

Rod rings
An important factor which affects casting range is the type of

rod rings on the rod. Rods with lined guides throughout have a far smaller opening for the line to travel through than snake guides, and will undoubtedly produce more resistance. When you consider the speed at which line runs through all ten or eleven rings, it adds up to a considerable difference. On the down side, rods fitted with cheap snake guides will wear flat spots in the wire surprisingly quickly; this produces a sharp edge which will soon ruin fly lines. If you are fitting snakes, always go for the best quality.

Tangling
Shooting head backing leaves a lot to be desired. I have yet to come across a backing which is tangle free - if I did, I would pay a good deal of money for it! The requirement for it to be light automatically makes it prone to tangle, but don't give up on your shooting head through frustration from this problem. I assure you that, with time and practice, the number of tangles will be greatly reduced.

Most beginners create tangles when they recast at the end of a retrieve. The last line retrieved will be the first line out during the next cast, so it is vitally important not to disturb the pile of line which has accumulated during the retrieve. An angler must lift the rod high above his head when recasting, and often the reel pulls on the line at the bottom of the pile, turning it over. Then the whole lot lifts up at once during the cast, resulting in a huge mess.

It may take some time to remember to pay attention to the line which is piling up in the line tray (or on the ground) during the retrieve, but doing so will greatly reduce the number of tangles. Always lay the first few yards of line of each new retrieve to one side before beginning the pile; this will prevent the next cast from disturbing it. The same applies if you are using a line tray. Always allow the first few yards of line to fall outside the basket, as this will enable you to make your next cast without disturbing the line in the basket.

Make your own shooting heads
Shooting heads can be quite expensive, especially when one considers that a shooting taper (ST) is only one third the length of a standard fly line, yet costs two thirds the price! In addition to this, casting finesse is not particularly important in fast sink shooting head work, so an expensive line affords little advantage over a cheap one. The most important issue is the sink rate, and cheap lines can sink just as fast as any others.

Years ago I read somewhere how to make shooting heads by purchasing a full length double tapered (DT) line and cutting the required length off each end, thereby making two tapered shooting heads from one full line. I decided to experiment, so I purchased a cheap, fast sink DT line from a catalogue. I was assured that it was just as fast sinking as the expensive makes and it cost me less than one sixth the price of the leading brand-ed make. I simply cut ten yards off each end, and attached a braided loop at each end of both lines. When I tried one, I couldn't detect any difference at all between it and my expensive branded shooting head.

Most regular users of shooting heads recommend that the heaviest line rating for the rod be chosen, or even one rating above the highest recommended. The standard length of a shooting head is ten yards, but it is advisable to cut it a little longer than this to start with. It is much easier to cut some off if it is too heavy than to add some if it is too light!

Weak link leaders
In chapter three I describe how to tie a heavy monofilament trace on the end of the leader to prevent the pike's teeth cutting the fine leader mono. Well, I must confess that I got lazy and began to use a single length of heavy line for the whole leader, instead of adding a couple of feet to the end as a trace. This was

a big mistake, and I am relating my sad story here so you won't do the same thing. If you hook up on the bottom with a 50lb leader, the backing will break before the leader breaks, resulting in the loss of the whole shooting head. I lost two before I learned my lesson! Using standard mono for the main part of the leader will provide a weak link, and if a snag-up occurs, only the fly and the trace will be lost. It takes a few extra seconds to tie up leaders like this, but it is well worth while, and permits a much more confident approach to any water.

Snap-offs and monofilament leaders
I have had an interesting time experimenting with monofilament pike traces, and there are significant differences in the performance of various types. My first departure from wire traces was with normal heavy monofilament of 30-40lb, and it was, at a pinch, an acceptable alternative. Changing flies took only a few seconds, and it did not kink up like wire, or add weight. Its only disadvantage was that it remained vulnerable to the pike's teeth, especially during a prolonged fight, and this continued to be a high risk problem until I discovered hard monofilaments.

Several of the larger UK mail order companies import these specialist leader materials from the USA, and they are substantially safer than regular heavy gauge mono. I began using 20lb Mason Hard Nylon (which is of equivalent thickness to 30 or 40lb regular monofilament) and it proved significantly better than ordinary mono. However, I continued to have frustrating problems with snap-offs from time to time during fights. These would occasionally occur without warning during a prolonged struggle (and a prolonged struggle always means a bigger fish!), and I was never completely confident in the material as a result. Risk of a snap-off depends on how the fish is hooked, and on how it fights. Obviously, if it is hooked in the lip and the head of the fly is clear of the mouth, the trace will suffer no chafing.

If the whole fly is in the mouth, the nylon will usually settle down between the teeth and will not be constantly subjected to the cutting effect of the pin-sharp teeth. Sometimes, a pike will open its mouth and shake its head violently, but this doesn't seem to do much harm either, though it is the most likely time during a fight for a snap-off to occur. The relatively small number of snap-offs during fights encouraged me to stick with Mason Hard monofilament instead of wire, but there was one surprising exception that really forced me to look for a better alternative.

I persistently suffered a very high number of snap-offs when fishing the surface, and all of them occurred as the fish took the fly. The first time it happened I lifted into a fish as it took the fly off the surface, fully expecting to feel a solid thump. Instead, the whole fly line came out of the water without any resistance, and I was amazed to discover the absence of my fly!' A close examination revealed a perfectly clean cut through the hard monofilament trace. This continued to happen on a regular basis when I was surface fishing, and the most curious feature was that very little resistance would be felt on the strike, yet the fly would still be gone. (It is also interesting that, in most cases, the fly appeared on the surface within seconds or minutes of the take, due to the pike ejecting it.)

Clearly, there is something about the way in which a fly is taken off the surface that, in certain circumstances, causes the line to be cut cleanly before the pike is hooked. I think this problem is due to the fact that, when surface fishing, the take can be seen by the angler before the fish actually gets hold of the fly, and sometimes the strike is made before the pike has closed its mouth tightly on the fly. This has the effect of drawing the line at speed across a whole row of needle sharp teeth, which results in a clean cut. Additionally, the pike will always turn downwards when it reaches the surface, and this movement also lends itself to a cutting action. I suspect that both of these factors contribute to causing the problem.

This prompted me to search for a better alternative, and the best material I have come up with so far is called Climax, and I now use it exclusively. Climax is used by saltwater fly fishermen in America for catching snook, a hard fighting fish with razor-sharp gill covers that will cut through ordinary monofilament leaders. Wire is an unsuitable alternative, because snook resolutely refuse to take a fly attached to wire - all pike anglers take note! Climax have developed this leader material to have a high shear resistance, and it is the only monofilament I would recommend for pike fishing. (See section on Traces in chapter 3 for details of where to purchase.)

Avoiding surface snap-offs
So far, I have suffered only a very few snap-offs with Climax, and all have occurred on the surface. (Out of several hundred fish, I think less than five is a very good safety record. It is also comforting to know that in every case the fly was returned immediately.) However, the urge to continually improve and refine has led me to experiment with a very difficult discipline - that of not striking when a fish takes. This amazing feat of self-control is familiar to the experienced salmon angler, but us trout anglers find it very hard to resist the compulsion to strike instantly at a surface take! It's worth learning, though, because dropping the rod for a second or two before tightening on the fish allows the pike to shut its mouth on the fly, and this effectively eliminates the risk of a snap-off.

Making wire traces
I must repeat myself: wire traces are a pain. Wire is heavy, highly visible, and very prone to kinking. But if it is to be used, go for the plastic coated variety, which will not kink up as quickly as uncoated wire. Coated wire, however, is seriously

handicapped by its thickness, which rules out knotting it to the fly. Crimping it to the fly leaves a very large and unsightly joint, to say nothing of the inconvenience, and snap links are just too large. This has always put me off using it, but a recent American development, called the melt knot, is both neat and very easy to tie, with the result that this kind of wire is now reasonably user friendly.

Using fifteen or twenty pound plastic-coated wire, thread the end through the eye of the fly and wind a short length of about one and a quarter inches back on itself, making seven or eight turns. Then heat it carefully with a cigarette lighter so that the plastic coating melts, fusing the knot. It is most important to make sure the plastic melts, but does not burn, as this may seriously weaken the connection. The knot is both quick to tie and fail-safe. I recently came across this leader system in Reynolds and Berryman's book 'Pike on the fly', and it is by far the easiest and best way to use wire. Just remember to bring wire cutters with you when you go fishing!

Weed guards

For anglers who intend to fish in weedy water, it is almost essential to use a fly with a built-in weed guard. It will transform your ability to fish among all kinds of weed without constantly getting caught up in it. A weed guard is simply a loop of heavy nylon which is tied in at the back of the hook bend, and the other end is tied in just behind the eye, so that the loop sits out proud of the hook point, as shown in the photograph. Stiff nylon is best, such as 20lb Mason Hard or Climax.

Tying a weed guard is very easy. Here's how. First cut off a four inch length of hard nylon, and flatten one end with pliers. Tie on 6\0 thread at the back of the shank, just where the bend starts. Lay a few turns, moving towards the point, and then offer the nylon up on the outside of the bend, with the flattened end up tight to the bed of thread. Continue laying the bed of thread over the nylon. The flattened end will assist in catching in the nylon, and leave a gradual rise instead of a sudden step. Tie in the nylon to the mid point of the bend and whip finish.

Catch the other end of the nylon in with a few turns, just behind the eye. (Don't forget to thread the foam head onto the shank first.) This will form a large loop of nylon around the hook bend, which can be reduced in size by pulling nylon through the tying at the eye. The ideal loop size should leave the nylon just sitting proud of the hook point. Finish by tying in tightly at the eye and trim off the excess.

Tip:- the nylon has a tendency to pull out through the tying, regardless of how tightly it is tied. This can easily be prevented by flattening the end of the nylon and then pulling it down into the tying until it jams tight. This will produce a stronger finish and will enable the tying to be kept small and neat. Also, cutting a small nick in the 'chin' of the foam head will help the head to sit up snugly to the eye.

Line trays - making your own is best
If you are going to wade, a line tray is essential if any decent casting range is to be achieved. I have only ever purchased one line tray, (a Bob Church model), but it leaves a lot to be desired.

I take great pleasure in experimenting with tackle in an attempt to improve it, and line trays are one tackle item where the home-made version can be better than anything you will buy in the shops. This is mainly due to the fact that most commercially made line trays are too small.

Making your own is both cheap and easy. All you need is an oblong shaped washing up basin and an adjustable strap. I use a one inch strap, which can be bought from any outdoor pursuits shop. Ideally, it should be about four feet in length, with a quick release\pull tight adjustment clip.

The first job is to remove the rim which runs all the way around the top. This is not essential, but I find it sits better against my body with the rim removed, as well as being lighter. A hack saw (or even a wood saw) will do the trick.

Once the rim is removed, the job is completed by making a few vertical slits for the strap. These should be made in one of the longer sides (assuming the basin is rectangular) starting about an inch from the top. Each slit should be exactly the same

length as the strap width for a snug fit. The easiest way to make them is to mark a line where the slit is required, and then drill a series of small holes close together along it. The remaining plastic can be chiselled out with a knife or with the drill to complete. The slits should be roughly nine inches apart for a comfortable fit against the body. The whole affair is then strapped around the waist, giving a deep and spacious line tray.

I have noticed that many commercially made line trays have a drain hole in the bottom to let any water that comes off the fly line escape, but I don't recommend it. A drain hole may seem like a good idea but it is not, because the tray will fill up with water if you are wading deep, rendering the tray useless. Besides, it takes hours to get enough water off the line to make any significant difference to your casting.

These rigid line trays are surprisingly comfortable to wear, and far better than anything you will buy. They are especially good for deep wading, because the tray will float on the water in front of you, rather than drowning, as many commercial trays do.

A good friend of mine, Jonny Phenix, has designed some very practical DIY line trays. The best one is made from a corrugated plastic box, which is extremely light, and Jonny sometimes straps it onto his thigh if he is strip retrieving. It will also collapse for easy transportation, and it is virtually indestructible. He has also made a super large line tray for use with solid mono backing. It is made from a nylon bait bucket used by coarse anglers, and is also excellent.

Pike fly wallet - how to make one
You can make a useful pike fly wallet with nothing more than a 'zipped' polythene bag and a piece of flexible foam. I use a bag of 6" x 9" with a flat piece of foam cut out about half an inch smaller than the bag's dimensions. Don't go for plastazote because it will not fold easily. Get larger cell foam which is soft

and pliable, about an eighth of an inch thick. Lay each fly on its side and stick the point and barb into the foam bed, but not through it. Make sure the flies are pointing in one direction and slip the whole 'tray' of flies into the bag, and seal the 'zipper'. You can fold it in half to fit neatly into a pocket, and the flies can be viewed without opening the bag. I usually run Sellotape along the edges of the bag to lengthen its life. Any wire traces on flies are wound around two fingers and secured in a neat loop to prevent tangling and kinking.

Ballydoolagh Bombers do not retain a lot of water, but if you have used half a dozen flies during a day's fishing, the bag can accumulate quite a bit of moisture. This will shorten the life of any fly and it is advisable to remove the tray at the end of the day to allow for drying. An alternative approach is to punch a few ventilation holes in the bag, using a file paper punch. These holes will help your flies keep fresh and dry without any extra attention.

Compound Shooting heads

When fishing on the bottom, a lot of time is spent waiting for the line to sink, and this time is largely wasted. Trout will sometimes take a fly on the way down (usually referred to as 'on the drop'), but pike rarely do. Therefore it is in the interests of the angler to get down to the fish as quickly as possible.

Fast sinking shooting heads leave a lot to be desired. Lines rated ultra fast sink (UFS) can be expensive, and some versions do not sink as fast as is claimed! On the other hand, while lead core lines are by far the fastest sinkers, they are not easy to cast or handle. I was taxed by this problem for some time, and over the years I have perfected a shooting head which combines the unmatched sink rate of lead core line with the user friendliness of normal fly line. I call it a Compound Shooting Head, because it is made from a combination of ordinary UFS fly line and lead core line.

I made my first compound shooting head using the long middle section of line from a full length UFS double taper. This line was the untapered section left over after I had made two shooting heads. (See 'Making your own shooting heads'.) I simply took seven yards of this and joined two and a half yards of lead core line to the front end.

Experimentation showed me that it takes about eighteen inches of lead core line to sink a Ballydoolagh Bomber, so seven or eight feet provides maximum sink rate without the necessity of a full lead core shooting head. Only the rear section of a shooting head is handled during the retrieve, so the user friendly qualities of ordinary fly line can be enjoyed along with the superfast sink rate of lead cores. Varying the lengths of each section of line will alter the casting qualities of the final product, and it is easy to experiment until the optimum balance is struck to suit the rod and the angler.

The compound ST line does not cast as well as a conventional ST, but it will cast a large fly such as the Ballydoolagh Bomber with ease.

In the following section, I will describe how to join two lengths of fly line so you can make your own.

How to join two lengths of fly line
(You can also use this trick to repair cut fly lines or to make your own sink tips.)

You will need-
Braided monofilament: a few feet will do. (Most makes of shooting head braided backing line are suitable.)
Superglue.
Fine thread.
Lighter or matches.
Nail clippers or scissors.

How braided connections work

If you take a short length of braided mono between your fingers and stretch it, it will tighten down into a slim diameter. However, if you compress it, it will widen out into a loose weave, becoming much larger in diameter, only tightening again when stretched. It is this action which makes braided mono suitable for attaching to fly lines. When compressed, it can easily be slid over the end of the fly line, but when it is pulled, it tightens around the fly line, gripping it ever more tightly as the pull increases. It is not the glue that provides the strength of the join, but this gripping action. The glue is applied only to stop the braid working itself off when slack. Understanding this will help you to produce good braided connections.

Making a braided joint

Cut off a nine inch length of braid and heat each end with a naked flame. This prevents the braid unravelling, but don't melt it too much so that the fly line cannot be inserted. Inserting a needle before applying the heat will help.

Compress one end and insert about four inches of fly line. Do the same at the other end, inserting the other length of fly line until it butts up to the first. Work the braid tight so that the lines sit butted up together.

Take about two feet of fine thread and begin whipping one end of the braid, about three inches back from where the two lines are butted up. Whip tightly for a length of about a quarter of an inch, keeping the tying slim and finishing with a simple knot. Lay a bed of superglue over the tying, and use nail clippers to cut off the excess inch or so of braid. Repeat at the other end of the joint. This will leave a six inch braided joint which will shoot smoothly, and give at least a whole season of reliable service. Do not glue the braid to the fly line anywhere between the whippings, as this will weaken the joint. A small piece of plastic tubing is often used instead of the whipping, but it will not shoot smoothly, nor is it as reliable.

This has proved to be both a fail-safe and long lasting connection.

Safe casting - use both hands
I touched on the subject of glasses earlier, and I would advise all anglers to wear them when casting large flies. Most fly fishing injuries occur when an angler has to cast with the wind blowing from the same side as their casting arm. The fly gets blown downwind on the forward cast and hits the angler in the face on the following back cast. Permanent damage can be inflicted to the face and eyes with these large hooks.

I have learned to cast equally well with both hands, and this makes fly fishing a lot safer, and means I don't need to wear glasses for protection as often as I might. I simply change my casting hand to the down wind side when circumstances demand it, thus rendering the cast completely safe. Knowing how to use both hands also pays huge dividends when casting in awkward spots or when trying to place a fly in a specific location, especially when the backcast is restricted.

Learning to cast with your other hand is not as difficult as it might sound. It will feel all wrong the first time you try it, but if you practice for ten minutes every time you go fishing you'll be amazed at how quickly you pick it up!

CHAPTER 16

PREPARING PIKE FOR THE TABLE

Before we start, I am aware that some anglers may object to this sort of chapter in an angling book on the grounds of conservation, but I would justify it by the fact that Ireland exports many tons of commercially caught pike each year for the table, and it is still an exceedingly plentiful resource here.

In some European countries, pike is a delicacy which often commands a higher price that either trout or salmon. But in Ireland the average person would not thank you for a freshly caught pike, even if it was prepared and ready to cook. In fact, many people here would refuse to eat pike under any circumstances - despite the fact that they would readily eat a trout which came from the same water!

Pike can be very enjoyable, and is both easy to prepare and cook. Of course, larger pike do not make such good eating as smaller fish, and I usually choose fish between three and six pounds for the table. I have also found that the taste will vary, depending on the water that the fish came from. I am not sure why this should be so, but I have noticed the same thing with trout.

Filleting
Cooking and eating your catch on a regular basis can become more trouble than it's worth, as I'm sure many trout anglers will agree! Going to the bother of gutting and scaling the fish, then wrapping the whole lot up in foil to cook for half an hour or more in the oven, followed by the fiddly business of skinning and boning the carcass - by which time the fish has gone cold - can become a chore. For years my freezer would be bursting at the seams by the end of the season with trout which were

gutted, but not filleted. After suffering this for a number of years, I decided to buy a filleting knife to see if I could improve the situation.

Hey, Presto! The results were amazing! After a little practice, filleting took less time than gutting, as well as being much cleaner, and the fillets took up much less space in the freezer. But the real advantage was the new versatility in cooking. My wife could prepare the fish in an endless variety of ways, and very soon we emptied the freezer out! We had never tried eating pike until I learned how to fillet, and it now features from time to time at family mealtimes instead of trout.

Filleting fish is easy once you know how, but it is a skill, and skill only comes with practice. My first attempt took me nearly half an hour, but I can now convert a whole pike into two lovely fillets in about five minutes. Here's how.

Lay the pike on its belly and holding a short, sharp knife with the point downwards, make an incision along the back from the head to the tail, cutting right down to the backbone. Be careful to keep to the same side of the backbone by feeling your way with the boning knife, keeping the blade tight to the bone.

Make a second cut parallel to the first, keeping to the other side of the backbone. Both incisions should run the entire length of the back and be about a centimetre apart.

Lay the pike on its side with the belly facing you. Slit open the belly from the vent right up to the throat. It is not necessary to remove the entrails.

With the fish still on its side, make a cut from top to bottom just behind the gill cover, in the soft flesh. This cut will join up with the cuts along the back and up the belly. Make a second top to bottom cut just forward of the tail. In both cases, cut right through the soft flesh to the bone.

Turn the pike around so the back is facing you, and angle the fish slightly towards your working hand. Using a sharp filleting knife, run it along the top cut in smooth, horizontal, flowing strokes, maintaining slight downward pressure to keep the knife near the bone. Cut over the backbone and past it, towards the belly. At this stage, you will have to cut through the fine pin bones, which grow out sideways from the spine. Keep the knife roughly flat but pressed slightly downwards onto the skeleton to ensure most of the meat comes away with the fillet instead of remaining on the carcass as you cut. Lift the loose flesh as you cut until the rib cage separates from the fillet and the remainder of the fillet comes away. Once the soft meat is separated from the carcase, the final job is to cut through the skin from the vent back to the tail. The fillet is now completely detached from the carcase.

Turn the fish over, and repeat the process on the other side. Remove the pelvic fins to complete.

The next step is to remove the skin. Take one fillet and lay it skin side down on a flat surface. Starting at the rear end, press four fingers and fingernails down onto the fillet as close to the end as possible. Using the filleting knife, make a cut just in front of your fingers, through the flesh to the skin. Do not cut through the skin; instead, turn the knife horizontal, and cut away from your fingers, between the skin and the flesh. Use a side to side, sawing action to cut. As you cut, keep moving your fingers in after the knife, pressing down as described. This keeps the skin from moving around and greatly assists in making a clean cut. Keep the knife dead flat to prevent cutting through the skin but at the same time keep it pressed down so that no meat will be left on the skin. Performing this task is much easier than it sounds, and with practice you will be able to make a clean separation of flesh and skin. Once separated, rinse the fillets under a cold tap.

Hints
It will take a few attempts to perfect the method so that a clean

fillet is produced. You will almost certainly make a complete mess of it on your first attempt but soon you will become familiar with the pike's innards and the job will become quicker and cleaner. Sharp knives are just about essential, and investing in a sharpening stone or an electric sharpener will make the whole job much easier.

When freezing, take care to keep the fillets separate as two fillets in the same bag will both have to be defrosted to be separated.

The average pike will produce two fillets weighing just under half its total weight, and, as a general rule, about 6 ounces of fish provides one adult portion.

Before cooking I always prepare the fillet in the following manner:-

Remove the frozen fillet from the bag by running under the cold tap. Fill a flat grill pan or baking dish with enough cold water to cover the fillet. Liberally salt the water, (several tablespoons) and place the fillet in the water to defrost and marinate. Defrosting will be complete in about ten or fifteen minutes, depending on how much water is in the pan and how warm it is. (Pour in some lukewarm water to speed things up if necessary.) Leave the fillet to soak in the water for half an hour to an hour. The salt will considerably enhance the flavour of the fish.

Recipes

There are endless recipes for fish, and pike can be used interchangeably with most other white fish. Using pike instead of salmon or trout in game fish recipes has also proved satisfactory. I have decided to include just two of our favourite recipes. These are both very tasty and very quick to prepare, which is partly why they are so popular!

Pike au gratin
Two fillets from a four pound pike.

4oz grated cheese.
2 tbl spoons of mayonnaise.
1 teaspoon paprika.
Serves four. Five minutes to prepare, ten minutes to cook.

Spread mayonnaise over one whole side of each fillet with the back of a spoon. Cover this with grated or thinly sliced cheddar cheese and sprinkle with paprika. Place under a grill, mark 3-4, (medium) for about ten minutes until the cheese is browned and the fish cooked.
Serve with boiled potatoes, vegetables and hot butter sauce.

Note: the pin bones are a row of fine bones which grow into the flesh along the spine. When filleting trout, these can be pulled out with tweezers, but the pin bones in a pike are exceptionally long and cannot be removed. Fortunately, they are easy to remove when eating, and most of them can be removed by dividing the fillet from top to bottom at several places. This will expose the bones and they can be easily pulled out.

Fish cakes
If you have a large stock of fish in your freezer it can be thawed, cooked and made into fish cakes which can be safely re-frozen. Fish cakes will make a healthy, impromptu meal in just a few minutes, and are very popular with children.

2lb of pike fillets
3lb boiled potatoes, peeled and mashed with a little butter.
Three egg yolks.
Several slices of brown bread
5 tea spoons dried parsley or 2 tbl spoons fresh chopped parsley.
1 medium onion.

Poach fillets until cooked. Remove pin bones by separating fillets from top to bottom and pulling out exposed bones.

Chop onion finely and lightly fry in a pan with a little oil. Mix fish, potato, parsley and fried onion together and season with salt and pepper, or to your own taste. Add egg yolk as required to bind the mixture and form it into cakes. The best way to do this is to shape the mixture into a log, (like a swiss roll) and cut it into cakes.

Place several slices of bread in a food processor to make bread-crumbs, (or purchase dried bread crumbs) and press cakes into the bread crumbs to coat. Place cakes in the freezer to store, or fry in shallow oil until golden brown.

Serve with just about anything.